UNLOCKING THE ECONOMIC AND SOCIAL VALUE OF INDONESIA'S STATE-OWNED ENTERPRISES

DECEMBER 2022

ADB

ASIAN DEVELOPMENT BANK

Notes:
In this publication, "$" refers to United States dollars and "Rp" refers to rupiah.

Cover design by Francis Joseph M. Manio.

On the cover: The view of Simpang Susun Semanggi Jakarta, Indonesia (photo by Sere Yordan Silaen/Shutterstock.com).

Contents

Tables, Figures, and Boxes

Foreword

Indonesia's state-owned enterprises (SOEs) have long played a key role in the economy of Indonesia as both commercial actors and as agents of government policy. Large SOEs are prominent in several crucial sectors including power generation and transmission, finance, telecommunications, transportation, and oil and gas, with many smaller SOEs further extending state participation in the economy into additional sectors. During the coronavirus disease (COVID-19) pandemic, SOEs have been active in supporting Indonesia's response to both the public health emergency as well as the resulting economic crisis. SOEs assisted with vaccine production and distribution, acted as conduits for economic stimulus, and helped cushion the blow of the pandemic for Indonesia's most vulnerable by providing necessary public goods. Going forward, SOEs have the potential to play an important role in addressing emerging megatrends such as technological disruption and climate change.

While the developmental and policy roles of SOEs are important, state intervention in, and competition with, the private economy comes with tradeoffs. SOEs can squeeze out private sector competition, the use of SOEs to achieve policy aims may be inefficient and increase costs while worsening delivery, and SOEs are often less dynamic than their private sector counterparts. In other contexts, similar challenges among SOEs have been linked to the difficulties of SOE governance, as SOEs exist in a unique regulatory space. With SOEs particularly prominent in the economies of many developing countries, figuring out this balance is critical to delivering economic progress. Aiming to minimize the potential disruptions that SOEs can create while maximizing their benefits must be an aim of Indonesia's SOEs' reform agenda, particularly given the need for a rapid economic recovery from the COVID-19 pandemic and the pressing development challenges faced by the country.

Over the past 2 decades, the Government of Indonesia has reshaped the nature of SOEs in the country, with increased public listing of state firms and improved governance and oversight within an improved legal framework. It has recently embarked on ambitious reforms of SOEs to further improve their performance and dynamism and enhance their economic and social benefit. The Ministry of State-Owned Enterprises is implementing reforms aimed at achieving a greater degree of consolidation of SOEs to better streamline management and increase focus on core activities, enhancing reporting and auditing quality, strengthening governance standards, and increasing the representation of women on SOE boards.

This report presents a comprehensive assessment of the SOE "ecosystem" in Indonesia, with an eye toward informing future reform efforts. By pursuing a broad array of reforms aimed at strengthening existing institutions and refining incentives, Indonesia can ensure its SOEs are able to deliver as both commercial and developmental entities. We hope that the findings of this report can help inform these reform efforts, and we look forward to continued engagement with all stakeholders on these important issues.

Ahmed M. Saeed
Vice-President for Southeast Asia,
East Asia, and the Pacific
Asian Development Bank

Acknowledgments

This diagnostic study on state-owned enterprises (SOEs) in Indonesia was prepared by the Asian Development Bank (ADB) as a knowledge product supporting SOEs' reform.

We would like to thank the senior management at the Ministry of State-Owned Enterprises. We are in particular thankful to Assistant Minister for Industry Rabin Hattari and Deputy for Finance and Risk Management Nawal Nely for providing guidance and support to the preparation of the study. We are also grateful to many officials at the Ministry of State-Owned Enterprises, the Ministry of Finance, other line ministries, as well as directors and chief executive officers at SOEs across a range of industries, including food, infrastructure, energy, technology, banking, health, and pharmaceuticals, among others. Their firsthand insights were invaluable in developing a deep understanding of the challenges and opportunities faced by SOEs in Indonesia.

The perspectives that experts shared greatly enriched the study and we thank the following for generously giving their time and sharing their thoughts: Vikram Nehru at Johns Hopkins University, Yougesh Khatri at Nanyang Technological University, David Nellor and Della Temenggung at Prospera, and Krystof Obidzinski at the Centre for International Forestry Research. We would also like to thank Fadli Rahman, Ronaldus Mujur, and Agustha Lumban for their comments and inputs to the study, and Mohamad Ikhsan and Richard Frederick for their peer review comments.

At ADB, we would like to thank Vice-President for Southeast Asia, East Asia, and the Pacific Ahmed M. Saeed; Vice-President for Knowledge Management Bambang Susantono; Ramesh Subramaniam, director general of the Southeast Asia Department (SERD); and Bruno Carrasco, director general of the Sustainable Development and Climate Change Department (SDCC) for their support. We are grateful for the guidance and support provided at various stages of the study by Winfried F. Wicklein, deputy director general, SERD; Jose Antonio Ramos Tan, director for Public Finance, SERD; and Jiro Tominaga, country director and Said Zaidansyah, deputy country director for the ADB resident mission in Indonesia.

The study also greatly benefited from the comments shared by our colleagues at ADB. For this we would like to thank Priasto Aji (senior economics officer, SERD), Kin Wai Chan (public–private partnership specialist, Office of Public–Private Partnership), David M. Dovan (senior investment specialist, Private Sector Operations Department), Anna M. Fink (country economist, SERD), Mohammed Azim Hashimi (principal public–private partnership specialist, Office of Public–Private Partnership), Florian Kitt (energy specialist, SERD), Henry Ma (senior country economist, SERD), Daniel Miller (senior finance specialist, SERD), Kaukab Naqvi (senior economist, Economic Research and Regional Cooperation Department), Thiam Hee Ng (director, South Asia Regional Department), Amr J. Qari (principal infrastructure specialist, SERD), and James P. Villafuerte (senior economist, SERD).

Yurendra Basnett, senior public management specialist at SERD, was the team leader of the study. David Robinett, senior public management specialist (State-Owned Enterprise Reforms), SDCC, provided guidance and support. Patrick Farrell (ADB consultant) carried out the economic analysis and drafting of the report. Cahyadi Indrananto (senior external relations officer, SERD) supported the report design and communications, while Jennalyn M. Delos Santos (operations assistant, SERD) supported the publication process. Andrew Fransciscus (programs officer, SERD), Marjorie Anne O. Javillonar (operations assistant, SDCC) and Anna Rini Hariandja (operations coordinator, SERD) provided operational support to the team.

Abbreviations

ADB	–	Asian Development Bank
BAPPENAS	–	Badan Perencanaan dan Pembangunan Nasional (National Development Planning Agency)
BPS	–	Badan Pusat Statistik (Statistics Indonesia)
COVID-19	–	coronavirus disease
GDP	–	gross domestic product
IDX	–	Indonesia Stock Exchange
IMF	–	International Monetary Fund
INA	–	Indonesia Investment Authority
IPO	–	initial public offering
MoF	–	Ministry of Finance
MSOE	–	Ministry of State-Owned Enterprises
PEN [plan]	–	Pemulihan Ekonomi Nasional (National Economic Recovery) plan
PLN	–	Perusahaan Listrik Negara (State Electricity Company)
PSO	–	public service obligation
ROA	–	return on asset
ROE	–	return on equity
SOE	–	state-owned enterprise

Executive Summary

State-owned enterprises (SOEs) have a prominent and longstanding presence in the Indonesian economy. SOEs have been a persistent target of reform efforts due to concerns regarding governance, misplaced incentives, risks of corruption, and the impact of SOEs on the macroeconomy. Substantial progress has been made on these fronts in Indonesia since the Asian financial crisis and democratization, with the creation of MSOE as a centralized authority overseeing SOEs, the listing of many SOEs on the stock exchange, and reforms and laws that have upgraded and formalized governance practices. However, many SOEs continue to face performance issues and financial pressures, while governance still lags behind international best practices in many respects.

This diagnostic study aims to inform the Government of Indonesia's SOEs' reform efforts, offering an overview of the current state of SOE governance and Indonesia's SOE ecosystem before providing an analysis of the economic and social role of SOEs. The study finds that SOEs achieve mixed performance in terms of economic and social value, facing distortions linked to governance shortcomings that limit SOE performance on both dimensions. Targeted reforms to ensure that SOEs deliver for Indonesia can help SOEs better drive economic development in Indonesia and support Indonesia's recovery from the coronavirus disease (COVID-19) pandemic.

State-Owned Enterprises in Indonesia: Overview and Governance

Overview of state-owned enterprises. The role and prominence of SOEs in the Indonesian economy has changed substantially over time, with the value of SOE assets in 2019 standing at over 56.2% of GDP, down from roughly 90% of GDP in 1990 but up from a trough of 36% of GDP in 2010. Similarly, SOE contribution to output has declined from roughly 13% in 1989 to an estimated 6% of output as of 2017. These shifts have also seen an increased emphasis on SOEs as commercial agents, with the majority of SOEs assets now belonging to state-owned commercial banks. The ownership of SOEs has also changed over time, with the majority of SOE assets belonging to partially state-owned firms as a result of listings on the stock exchange. SOEs continue to operate in many sectors, with large SOEs operating in sectors including energy, banking, pension funds, telecommunications, mining, and fertilizer, with smaller SOEs in sectors as varied as film production and hospitality.

Governance of state-owned enterprises. The institutions and laws of SOE governance in Indonesia have improved in line with international best practices in many aspects since the Asian financial crisis, but governance shortcomings remain. The MSOE exercises much of the state's ownership function but faces capacity and capability constraints while also intervening frequently in SOE operations. Other line and technical ministries also impact SOEs through regulations they set as well as their role in assigning public service obligations (PSOs), the public goods and services provided by SOEs to fulfill government policy aims. The Ministry of Finance, which maintains ultimate ownership of SOE assets, is responsible for compensating SOEs for PSOs, approving changes in ownership, setting dividend levels, and itself exercises direct control of some state companies. This creates a scattered SOE ecosystem, contributing to coordination problems that negatively impact SOE performance as both commercial entities and as agents of government policy. Application of the SOE Law—which sets SOE governance standards—to the full SOE ecosystem is incomplete because key regulations, such as those on boards, are imperfectly applied to SOE subsidiaries.

Assessing State-Owned Enterprises: Economic and Social Value

Economic value. The commercial performance of SOEs is mixed; some SOEs perform well while many others lack commercial viability. Reforms since the Asian financial crisis, such as partial public listings of SOEs, likely contributed to improved commercial performance.
- Roughly one-third of SOEs lack commercial viability, but when excluding the Perusahaan Listrik Negara (the State Electricity Company, or PLN), which has a unique public service role, unviable SOEs account for a comparatively small fraction of SOE assets (Figure 5).
- While many large SOEs are viable, their performance tends to lag compared to private firms, with SOEs in many sectors performing worse than the emerging market sector average (Figure 6).
- Public listing of SOE shares may help improve SOE performance in Indonesia; while it is difficult to prove causality, there is suggestive evidence that public listing is associated with improved SOE performance in the years after an initial public offering or sale (Table 2).
- The mixed commercial performance of SOEs can be attributable to several factors, including the pressures of PSOs, management limitations, and the limited independence of SOEs (paras. 32 and 33).

Social value. As SOEs are also often relied upon as agents of development, they must also be assessed in terms of their contribution to social value. SOEs are key providers of public goods in Indonesia but some policies introduce costly market distortions.
- The provision of PSOs through SOEs to achieve policy aims has been a longstanding rationale for state involvement in the economy (para. 34).
- Infrastructure construction by SOEs has been particularly prominent in recent years, with SOEs now accounting for roughly a third of infrastructure investment, and large injections of equity capital have been used to increase the size of infrastructure SOEs (para. 35).
- Other low prices for some public goods, most notably energy, fuel, and fertilizer, are compensated with production subsidies to allow SOEs to provide goods at below market rates. The targeting of these subsidies is imperfect, with a large share of the benefits going to unintended recipients (para. 36).
- The compensation of SOEs through production subsidies and equity injections create strains for SOEs while also limiting the potential for private sector participation in the provision of these goods (paras. 35 and 36).
- Persistent uncompensated costs borne by SOEs that manifest in lower than anticipated performance, which can be viewed as "implicit subsidies" from the government to SOEs, are large and growing (para. 37).
- The overall impact of SOEs on the budget is difficult to assess, given the many hidden costs and distortions in the economy created by state ownership (para. 38).

Constraints to State-Owned Enterprises Performance, Current Reforms, and Additional Proposed Reforms

The MSOE is currently pursuing a broad reform agenda, including the reorganization of the MSOE itself, continued consolidation of SOEs, and improvements to SOE governance such as the adoption of heightened standards and greater standardization. There is room to build on this progress to help ensure SOEs deliver as both commercial entities and providers of social value.

This report proposes reforms to address the constraints facing SOEs, building on the current efforts of the MSOE. Given the institutions of SOE governance in Indonesia and the challenges facing Indonesia's SOEs, this diagnostic outlines reforms grouped into three "pillars":

- Pillar 1: Reforms to the MSOE
- Pillar 2: Reforms to SOE–government relations
- Pillar 3: Reforms to SOEs

Pillar 1: Reforms to the Ministry of State-Owned Enterprises. The MSOE should upgrade its capacity and capabilities to better fulfill its mandate. The MSOE should aim to focus on improving SOE governance and limiting interventions in SOE operations, while increasing hiring standards and boosting personnel capacity within MSOE alongside efforts to improve the availability and quality of data on SOEs.

Constraints		Proposed Reforms
Existing poor governance practices and need for more focus on primary mission of encouraging good governance practices	→	Align governance standards with best practices and increase the MSOE's focus on ensuring good governance practices
The MSOE lacks the necessary capacity and capabilities to carry out its mission	→	Increase the MSOE's capacity and capability by acquiring external talent, accelerating talent development, and establishing formalized training programs
The MSOE lacks complete data on many aspects of the SOE ecosystem, particularly SOE subsidiaries	→	Upgrade MSOE data practices and technological capabilities

Pillar 2: Reforms to state-owned enterprise–government relations. More coordination and regular cross-ministry dialogue should be encouraged to ensure engagement on PSOs and other regulations that impact SOEs. PSO compensation for many subsidies should be adjusted to avoid creating poor incentives and locking out private sector firms from government projects. The government should form an inter-ministerial PSO advisory committee consisting of Ministry of Finance, MSOE, and relevant technical line ministries to drive improvements to PSO compensation.

Constraints		Proposed Reforms
Misalignments, lack of coordination with line or technical ministries lead to inefficiencies	→	Formalize regular engagement and consultations with technical ministries and the Ministry of Finance on PSO compensation structures and strategy
PSO compensation structure limits private sector participation in government projects, economy	→	Reform PSO compensation by moving to incentive-compatible subsidy structures and the use of viability-gap funding mechanisms for infrastructure PSOs
PSOs are often poorly structured, increasing both their long-term cost and their impact on SOEs	→	Create a PSO-advisory committee within the MSOE to assist officials in negotiating PSO compensation structures

Pillar 3: Reforms to state-owned enterprises. To increase SOE performance and competitiveness, unviable SOEs should be closed or consolidated and commercially viable SOEs should be publicly listed to introduce more market incentives. Indonesia's successful SOEs could benefit from better and more stable leadership, and SOE boards should be improved while also taking on increased responsibilities for SOE performance and planning.

Constraints		Proposed Reforms
Many SOEs are not commercially viable, and consolidations often are limited in impact	→	Consolidate SOEs to streamline business focus and close unviable, unnecessary SOEs
Several SOEs lack a clear rationale for state ownership, should face market incentives	→	Encourage at least partial nonstate ownership of commercially viable SOEs through initial public offerings/sales
SOEs lack independence and capable management	→	Improve the quality of SOE leadership and give SOE boards more independence while increasing accountability for SOE performance

Conclusion

SOEs have the potential to act as agents of development to help tackle the many pressing issues Indonesia faces, such as building much-needed infrastructure, catalyzing private investment, preparing for the impacts of climate change, and encouraging technological upgrading. To help Indonesia's SOEs deliver on this potential, alleviating several of the constraints that have hindered SOE performance while upgrading SOE governance will be critical. Ensuring that Indonesia's SOEs deliver as both providers of economic and social value for Indonesia can help set the stage for Indonesia's recovery from the COVID-19 pandemic and support continued development progress.

I. Introduction

1.   State-owned enterprises (SOEs) have a prominent and longstanding presence in the Indonesian economy.[1] As of 2021, there were over 100 SOEs in Indonesia overseen by the Ministry of State-Owned Enterprises (MSOE). These SOEs are comprised of over 1,000 subsidiaries and hold more than $500 billion (Rp8,892 trillion) in assets—equivalent to 56.2% of the country's gross domestic product (GDP) in 2019—and account for roughly 6% of Indonesian output (as of 2017).[2] While these figures are smaller than those in regional peer countries, SOEs play an influential role in several key sectors of the economy of Indonesia, such as in power generation and transmission, finance, telecommunications, transportation, and oil and gas.[3] Several large SOEs in Indonesia function largely as commercial enterprises and are among the top Indonesian companies. Some SOEs have been frequently relied upon as agents of government policy and act on a noncommercial basis for social benefit, while others are nonviable entities that are difficult to shut down due to political constraints.

2.   SOEs have frequently been the targets of reform efforts due to concerns regarding governance, misplaced incentives, risks of corruption, and the impact of SOEs on the macroeconomy.[4] Substantial progress has been made on these fronts with the creation of new institutions, the listing of many SOEs on the stock exchange, and reforms that have upgraded governance practices. However, many SOEs continue to face performance challenges and financial pressures, while governance still lags behind international best practices in many respects. SOEs have the potential to act as agents of development to tackle the many pressing issues Indonesia faces, such as building much-needed infrastructure, catalyzing private investment, preparing for the impacts of climate change, and encouraging technological upgrading. However, state ownership and involvement in the economy should have a clearly defined rationale and must be conditioned with the proper incentives to ensure that SOEs provide economic and social benefit.

---

[1]   This study focuses on SOEs owned by the central government, in line with the Asian Development Bank (ADB) definition of an SOE as a "legal entity established to undertake commercial activities and owned fully or largely by the sovereign." ADB. 2018. *State-Owned Enterprise Engagement and Reform*. Manila. Most SOEs are overseen by the MSOE, and these entities are the focus of the report. A small number of enterprises owned by the central government are fully overseen by the Ministry of Finance and are discussed in this report as well, but are not included in the analysis focused on SOEs overseen by the MSOE. There are also regional and local government-owned entities in Indonesia, which are not the focus of this report. However, the report's recommendations to ensure improved governance for SOEs extend to these entities as well.

[2]   Calculations based on MSOE data accessed in 2020. Source of share of output estimate is E. Ginting and K. Naqvi, eds. 2020. *Reforms, Opportunities, and Challenges for State-Owned Enterprises*. Manila: ADB. Given the enormous impact of COVID-19 on the economy, the study uses SOE financial data up to 2019 in the analysis and separately reports the latest data as relevant.

[3]   SOE contribution to GDP is estimated to be 25% of GDP in India, 30% in the People's Republic of China, 25% in Thailand, and 38% in Viet Nam, compared to 6%–8% in Indonesia. E. Ginting and K. Naqvi, eds. 2020. *Reforms, Opportunities, and Challenges for State-Owned Enterprises*. Manila: ADB.

[4]   A. Wicaksono. 2008. Indonesian State-Owned Enterprises: The Challenge of Reform. *Southeast Asian Affairs*. pp. 146–167; World Bank. Infrastructure Sector Assessment. Unpublished; Australia Indonesia Partnership for Economic Governance (AIPEG). Implicit Subsidies to Indonesia's SOEs are Creating Significant Risks to Indonesia's Economy. Unpublished.

3.   The economic crisis resulting from the coronavirus disease (COVID-19) pandemic has increased the urgency of reform, with SOEs being called upon to play a key role in Indonesia's public health and fiscal response. A portion of Indonesia's fiscal stimulus has been executed through support to SOEs, and SOEs have also been called upon to support the Government of Indonesia's public health response, developing new technological solutions and distributing vaccines.[1] In addition to the need for reforms in the context of the COVID-19 pandemic and Indonesia's economic recovery, the MSOE is receptive to reform under a new, reform-minded minister, who has restructured the MSOE and appointed professionals with substantial private sector experience to the ministry and to SOE management.

4.   This study aims to inform the government's SOEs' reform efforts. It builds on the insights provided by a recent cross-country SOE assessment by the Economic Research and Regional Cooperation Department of the Asian Development Bank (ADB).[6] Informed by international best practices, this diagnostic study identifies three key pillars of reform actions to maximize SOEs' performance, both as commercial enterprises and as agents of development: (i) reforms to the MSOE; (ii) reforms to SOE–government relations; and (iii) reforms to SOEs themselves (Figure 1). Given pronounced capacity constraints within the MSOE, increasing MSOE performance is critical for successful reform. The government's relationship with SOEs and the use of SOEs for developmental aims must be reformed to ensure that SOEs are properly compensated, and that state ownership does not provide SOEs with an advantage when competing with private firms. SOEs themselves must also be made more competitive and more independent by limiting state intervention or, in cases where intervention is unavoidable, mitigating the impact of state intervention, in line with best practices.

Figure 1: Diagnostic Framework for State-Owned Enterprises' Reform

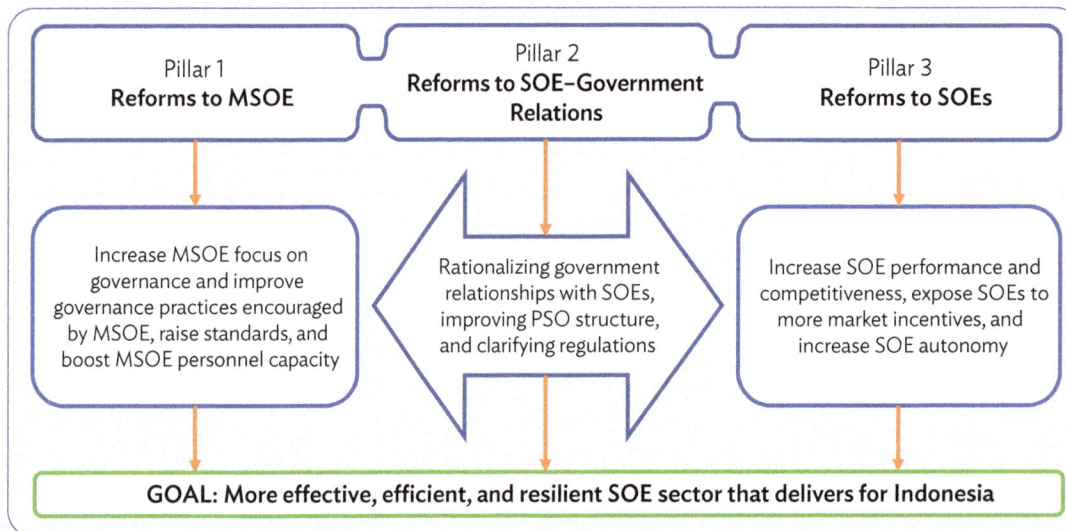

MSOE = Ministry of State-Owned Enterprises, PSO = public service obligation, SOE = state-owned enterprise.

Source: Asian Development Bank.

---

[1]   Government of Indonesia, Ministry of Finance. 2020. *BUMN Juga Masuk Program Pemulihan Ekonomi Nasional (SOEs Are Also a Part of the National Economic Recovery Program)*. Jakarta.

[6]   ADB. 2008. *Completion Report: State-Owned Enterprise Governance and Privatization Program in Indonesia*. Manila.

5.   Pillar 1 recommendations include increasing the MSOE's focus on ensuring good governance practices while discouraging interventions in SOEs, increasing the capacity and capability of MSOE, and upgrading data practices. For Pillar 2, recommendations include ensuring SOE noncommercial activities are properly structured and compensated, increasing MSOE engagement with the many ministries that impact SOEs, and establishing a new advisory committee focused on SOE public service obligations (PSOs) within the MSOE. Within Pillar 3, recommendations include encouraging further consolidation of SOEs while seeking to unwind or close down unviable SOEs, encouraging at least partial nonstate ownership of SOEs, and enabling increased SOE autonomy. A more capable and more focused MSOE that aims to ensure good governance practices, complemented by reformed compensation structures for PSOs, and alongside more independent, better-managed, and market-driven SOEs can help ensure that SOEs deliver both economic and social value for Indonesia.

6.   The analysis and recommendations contained in this diagnostic study, particularly the recommendation to refocus the MSOE on its central governance mission, can help advance President Joko Widodo's aim of simplifying the bureaucracy as emphasized in his second inaugural address and subsequent statements.[7] The report is aligned with the priorities of the government's National Medium-Term Development Plan 2020–2024 (RPJMN), which emphasizes the need to "increase the capacity, capability, and competitiveness of SOEs," and the aims of Vision of Indonesia 2045.[8] This report also aims to provide insights on Indonesian SOEs that can aid ADB-supported programs undertaken under the country partnership strategy (CPS), 2020–2024, which emphasizes the importance of SOEs' reform in Indonesia.[9] This report is informed by ADB's prior experience with SOEs' reform in Indonesia, as well as independent evaluation of ADB projects relating to SOEs' reform[10] The report reflects ADB strategy for SOEs' reform in ADB's Strategy 2030 and recent ADB guidance on SOEs' reform.[11]

7.   This diagnostic study begins by discussing SOE governance in Indonesia and its development. The role and prominence of SOEs in the Indonesian economy are discussed in Section II, while Section III assesses the performance of SOEs in terms of both economic and social value. Section IV outlines the ongoing SOEs' reform agenda in Indonesia and the current economic context. Section V discusses the constraints identified as holding back SOE performance and suggests additional reforms to ensure SOEs in Indonesia provide both economic and social benefit. Section VI concludes the diagnostic study.

---

7   *The Jakarta Post.* 2019. Jokowi's Full Inaugural Speech. Jakarta; Government of Indonesia, Cabinet Secretariat. 2020. President Jokowi Pushes for Simplification of Bureaucracy. Jakarta.

8   Government of Indonesia. 2019. *National Medium-Term Development Plan 2020–2024.* Jakarta. The original text is "...[M]eningkatkan kapasitas, kapabilitas serta daya saing BUMN."

9   ADB. 2020. *Country Partnership Strategy: Indonesia, 2020–2024—Emerging Stronger.* Manila.

10   ADB. 2018. *State-Owned Enterprise Engagement and Reform.* Manila.

11   ADB. 2021. *Guidance Note on State-Owned Enterprise Reform in Sovereign Projects and Programs.* Manila; ADB. 2018. *Strategy 2030: Achieving a Prosperous, Inclusive, Resilient, and Sustainable Asia and the Pacific.* Manila.

II. Overview of State-Owned Enterprises and their Governance in Indonesia

8.   SOEs play a prominent and evolving role in the Indonesian economy. SOEs act as commercial entities, agents of development, and sources of government revenue. SOEs' reform in Indonesia has sought to strengthen governance to improve performance, as reform efforts internationally have highlighted that poor SOE performance is often linked to governance issues. A poorly defined rationale for state ownership, divergent and contradictory mandates, misaligned incentives, politicized selection of management, and a lack of autonomy, among other issues, can limit SOE performance.[12] Within proper governance frameworks, SOEs can perform as well as comparable private firms.[13] The impact of SOEs' reform in the Indonesian context has been positive, but further reforms, tailored to local institutions and the challenges facing Indonesia's SOEs, are necessary.

9.   Since the Asian financial crisis, Indonesia has made substantial improvements to SOE governance. Key reforms included the enactment of an updated legal framework and the creation of new institutions to oversee SOEs (paras. 10 and 14). The creation of the MSOE, a dedicated institution exercising the state's ownership role, improved governance by centralizing many aspects of oversight and ownership. The listing of many SOEs on the stock exchange helped to introduce additional market incentives for performance, and the consolidation of many SOEs into holding companies has helped to reduce the overall number of SOEs and better focus their commercial activities (paras. 24 and 26). SOEs are subject to the same accounting and audit standards as locally listed companies, with local standards for financial disclosure requirements largely aligned with International Financial Reporting Standards (IFRS).[14] Still, some aspects of Indonesia's SOE governance framework require improvements to align with international good practices, including those established by the Organisation for Economic Co-operation and Development (OECD). In particular, the capacity constraints of the MSOE, the fragmentation in SOE oversight, and the level of independence of SOE boards in many respects leave room for further progress. Oversight of SOE subsidiaries is a challenge, given the shortage of reliable data on subsidiaries and limited application of key provisions of the SOE Law to these entities. In addition, while the number of publicly traded SOEs has increased, full divestments and closures have been rare as a result of political economy constraints.

A. Overview of State-Owned Enterprise Governance in Indonesia

10.   **Laws and regulations.** The three primary laws impacting SOEs are the State Finance Law (17/2003), the SOE Law (19/2003), and the 2004 Treasury Law (1/2004). While many other laws and regulations also impact SOEs, these three play a particularly prominent role in establishing the context in which SOEs operate.

---

[12]   World Bank. 2014. *Corporate Governance of State-Owned Enterprises: A Toolkit.* Washington, DC.

[13]   H. J. Chang. 2007. State-Owned Enterprise Reform. *National Development Strategies Policy Note.* United Nations Department for Economic and Social Affairs.

[14]   Organisation for Economic Co-operation and Development (OECD). 2020. *Transparency Frameworks for SOEs in Asia.* Paris.

- **State Finance Law.** First proposed in 2000 in the wake of the Asian financial crisis and passed in 2003, this law is intended to establish a sound system of public finance management in Indonesia.[15] The law sets a cap on the central government budget deficit (3% of GDP) and limits on the overall debt-to-GDP ratio, which Indonesia has largely adhered to since (the deficit cap has been lifted during the COVID-19 crisis). The deficit cap has been praised by many international financial institutions for encouraging budget discipline.[16] However, it also incentivizes the use of SOEs to reduce on-budget spending, by shifting spending and borrowing onto SOE balance sheets, and limits the government's fiscal space to compensate SOEs for PSOs.
- **State-Owned Enterprises Law**. This law, passed in 2003, establishes the current legal framework for SOEs in Indonesia (para. 11), and sets out the responsibilities of boards of directors and commissioners (para. 13). It also prohibits the privatization of SOEs in defense and natural resources as well as those SOEs that execute "special tasks related to the public interest."[17] This law sets out a requirement that privatization must be agreed upon by a Privatization Committee that brings together the coordinating minister for Economic Affairs, SOE minister, finance minister, and technical ministers and other officials as necessary, with privatization requiring consultation with the House of Representatives. The SOE Law largely aligns with international best practices, but application of the law to subsidiaries has been incomplete.
- **Treasury Law**. This law is primarily focused on the management of state funds, and impacts SOEs as they operate using state assets. The law increases the scope of possible liability risk faced by SOEs by requiring that "state losses," a broadly defined term that has sometimes been applied to losses of state assets, be recorded and specifies that state officials may be legally liable for these losses.[18] The elucidation of the act specifies that this liability may extend to employees of SOEs, making SOE employees potentially liable for company losses and increasing the risk aversion of SOEs.

11.   **Types and purpose of state-owned enterprises.** Under the SOE Law, SOEs are organized into two main types, *persero* and *perum,* that have different structures and legally defined purposes.

- **Persero**. From *perseroan*, these are a type of limited liability company (*perseroan terbatas*, or PT). The capital of these SOEs has been divided into shares of which at least 51% is owned by the state. As defined in the SOE Law, the primary objective of these firms is commercial. These SOEs may have mixed ownership structures, with many currently listed on the Jakarta Stock Exchange. The names of firms currently traded on exchanges include Tbk, from *terbuka* (open). *Persero* operate under regulations that apply to private limited liability companies (Law No. 40/2007).[19]
- **Perum**. From *perusahaan umum* (public company). As defined in the SOE Law, *perum* are intended to conduct business on behalf of the public interest while also pursuing profit. The capital of *perum* are not divided into shares. The articles of association for *perum* are defined through government regulations. All *perum* are fully state-owned, though they may have subsidiaries that are not fully state-owned.

12.   **Ambiguity in the delineation of SOE types.** The legal status of SOEs can be identified in their corporate name, such as the state power company PT Perusahaan Listrik Negara (Persero) (PLN), a *persero* that is not publicly traded; the toll road operator PT Jasa Marga (Persero) Tbk, a publicly traded *persero*; or the forestry management company Perum Perhutani, a *perum*. While the law draws a distinction between SOEs intended

---

[15]   Government of Indonesia. 2003. State Finance Law (17/2003). Jakarta; E. Ginting. 2003. The State Finance Law: Overlooked and Undervalued. *Bulletin of Indonesian Economic Studies.* 39 (3). pp. 353–357.
[16]   L. E. Breue, J. Guajardo, and T. Kinda. 2018. *Realizing Indonesia's Economic Potential.* International Monetary Fund (IMF); IMF. 2019. Article IV Consultation 2019. Washington, DC.
[17]   Government of Indonesia. 2003. SOE Law (19/2003). Jakarta.
[18]   Government of Indonesia. 2004. Act of the Republic of Indonesia (1/2004) Concerning State Treasury. Jakarta.
[19]   R. Januarita. 2010. *Equal Opportunities between SOEs and Private Companies.* Bandung: OECD.

to pursue commercial aims and those that act in the public interest, in practice this distinction is blurry and often not followed. PLN, for example, is a *persero* but operates as a public service provider of electricity at a "reasonable price to improve public welfare," receiving subsidies to sell electricity below the cost of production. The delineation of the two types of SOEs has been further blurred by reorganizations that have structured some *persero* as subsidiaries of *perum*. Of the 114 SOEs in 2019, 13 were *perum* and 101 were *persero*, of which 16 were publicly listed. *Persero* accounted for 99.1% of all SOE assets in 2019; the 16 publicly listed *persero* accounted for 54.0% of all SOE assets. The lack of a clear delineation of the two types of SOEs, in many cases due to consolidations, along with the small size of *perum* relative to *persero* may merit reform to simplify and standardize the legal status of SOEs.

13.   **Corporate structure and boards of state-owned enterprises.** Indonesian corporate governance structures include both a board of directors and a board of commissioners. This structure applies to both private firms and SOEs, as defined under the SOE Law (footnote 17). Boards of directors oversee the day–to–day operations of SOEs, and independent boards of commissioners are tasked with the supervision of the board of directors.[20] The quality and independence of SOE boards in Indonesia varies and is of concern, particularly given the importance of SOE boards which play an important role in the day–to–day operations of SOEs. Remuneration of independent commissioners, who play a key oversight role, has been criticized as below market rates, creating difficulties in finding talent to fill these roles.[21] In addition, while members of SOE boards (both commissioners and directors) are in theory required to be independent of the government, this requirement is often not well-enforced.[22] Of particular concern is the limited application of the SOE Law to SOE subsidiaries. As disclosure requirements for subsidiaries are weak and the application of the SOE Law to subsidiaries is incomplete, commissioners and directors of SOE subsidiaries are often political figures or retired former directors of parent SOEs, which undermines their independence.[23] Improving SOE performance will require addressing shortcomings on boards and ensuring board quality, autonomy, and independence for all SOEs and SOE subsidiaries.

14.   **Institutions of government ownership.** From the 1960s until 1998, SOE management was shared between the Ministry of Finance (MoF) and relevant sector ministries, with planning input from the National Development Planning Agency (BAPPENAS).[24] To centralize SOE management, a ministry-level entity was created in 1998 under President B. J. Habibie before being dissolved in 2000 following a cabinet reorganization under President Abdurrahman Wahid and reformed as the MSOE in 2001, after the inauguration of President Megawati Sukarnoputri.[25] In its early years, mirroring the political changes of the period of democratization, the MSOE was characterized by a lack of stability; it had five different ministers from 1998 to 2007.[26] Still, the creation of the MSOE is viewed as having played a positive role in improving Indonesia's SOE governance (footnote 12). Many other institutions continue to influence SOE governance, including the MoF as well as sector and coordinating ministries (paras. 17 and 18), with the MoF being the ultimate owner of SOE assets and playing a key budget support function for SOEs and the sector and coordinating ministries heavily influencing the developmental role of SOEs through their role in setting prices and overseeing subsidies.

---

[20]   J. Yap, D. Tan, and L. Z. Yong. 2020. Corporate Governance In Indonesia – What You Need To Know About The Board Of Directors And Board Of Commissioners. *Mondaq*. 26 March.

[21]   S. A. Sari and T. F. Tjoe. 2017. Board Remuneration and Good Corporate Governance in Indonesian State-Owned Enterprises. *Global Business Review*. 18 (4). pp. 861–875. 15 May.

[22]   F. G. Worang and D. A. Holloway. 2007. Corporate Governance in Indonesian State-Owned Enterprises. *Journal of Corporate Ownership & Control*. 4 (2). pp. 205–215.

[23]   K. Kim. 2018. Matchmaking: Establishment of State-Owned Holding Companies in Indonesia. *Journal of Asia & The Pacific Policy Studies*. 10 May.

[24]   M. Indreswari. 2006. Corporate Governance of Indonesian State-Owned Enterprises.

[25]   Government of Indonesia, MSOE. 2020. Profil Organisasi (Organization Profile). Jakarta.

[26]   A. Wicaksono. 2008. Indonesian State-Owned Enterprises: The Challenge of Reform. *Southeast Asian Affairs*. pp. 146–167.

15.   **The model of state-owned enterprise governance in Indonesia.** SOE oversight in Indonesia can be best characterized by a dual-ownership model (Box 1), with elements of decentralization and multiple centers of control still evident in Indonesia's SOE oversight framework.[27] The MSOE exercises many, but not all, aspects of the state's ownership function, with the MoF being the ultimate owner of state assets and also exercising ownership of some SOEs. Further, line and sector ministries continue to have substantial influence on the performance of many SOEs. While the presence of a centralized ministry or institution is viewed as a way to reduce political intervention, interventions into SOEs have remained frequent in Indonesia even after the introduction of the MSOE. These problems represent two key issues regarding Indonesia's SOE governance: (i) there is a high degree of fragmentation, with many ministries impacting SOEs and (ii) the MSOE frequently intervenes in the day–to–day operations of its holdings. Ensuring that Indonesia's SOE governance framework conforms to international best practices will require limiting fragmentation, in line with the OECD's recommendation to centralize the state's ownership function (Box 1), and ensuring that the MSOE acts to address existing governance shortfalls and refocus on its oversight function, rather than continuing its active interventions in the operations of its holdings.

16.   **Role of the Ministry of State-Owned Enterprises.** The MSOE is a unique ministry, tasked with developing and enacting government policy and overseeing profit-driven commercial entities. The MSOE performs several functions. It represents the government in SOE shareholder meetings, where it exercises its authority to make appointments to the boards of directors and commissioners, approve annual accounts, oversee strategic and annual planning, approve annual budgets, and select an audit firm, among other actions as required of a shareholder by the articles of association and situation of each SOE. The MSOE plays an active role in the oversight of SOEs, monitoring quarterly performance, providing approval for certain actions and investments, and working with SOEs to establish agreements for PSO provision.

17.   **The continued role of the Ministry of Finance.** Despite the existence of a ministry overseeing SOEs, several aspects of state ownership in the economy are still overseen by the MoF. In many respects, the MSOE has historically been subsidiary to the MoF. Until 2018, over 80% of MSOE staff were officially employees of the MoF and not the MSOE. Further, SOE assets are owned by the MoF and managed by the MoF's Directorate General of State Asset Management, meaning that while the MSOE is authorized to represent the government at shareholder meetings, it does not have legal ownership of SOE assets. Dividends that SOEs pay on government-held shares are received by the MoF, and the MoF is involved in setting dividend request targets. The MoF is also responsible for paying subsidies and compensating SOEs for PSOs, but payment delays are common and create uncertainty for SOEs, straining their balance sheets.[28] The MoF also exercises full ownership of several SOEs, largely ones closely linked to financial stability and investment guarantees.[29] These SOEs include PT Sarana Multi Infrastruktur (SMI), PT Penjaminan Infrastruktur Indonesia (PII), and PT Sarana Multigriya Finansial (SMF), all of which are primarily noncommercial financial SOEs (in contrast with the more commercially focused SOE banks, which are overseen by the MSOE). Additionally, PT Geo Dipa Energi (GDE) is a renewable energy SOE that is currently managed by the MoF rather than the MSOE following a transfer to the MoF for restructuring. The assets of the four MoF SOEs totaled Rp117 trillion in 2019, or roughly 1.3% of the Rp8,892 trillion in assets of the SOEs overseen by the MSOE.[30]

---

[27]   Asian Development Bank Institute. 2020. *Enhancing the Transparency and Accountability of SOEs.* Tokyo.
[28]   *Fitch Ratings.* 2020. Compensation Delays to Pressurise PLN's Standalone Credit Profile. New York.
[29]   Due to the unique nature of the MoF SOEs and limited available data, these SOEs are not included in the set of SOEs considered elsewhere in this report.
[30]   ADB calculation based on MSOE data, SOE annual reports.

Box 1: International Perspectives on State-Owned Enterprise Ownership Structures

The institutional structures of state-owned enterprise (SOE) governance can be broadly divided into the following five categories:[a]

- **Centralized model.** A holding company or a central coordinating body responsible for monitoring performance or coordinating governance practices across the SOE sector.
- **Coordinating agency.** A specialized government agency operating in an advisory capacity to other shareholding ministries on operation and technical issues, with a policy mandate to monitor SOE performance.
- **Dual-ownership.** When two ministries or institutions both exercise ownership functions of an SOE, often comprising a line ministry along with a ministry tasked with overall SOE performance monitoring.
- **Twin-track.** Similar to the centralized model, but with an SOE sector split into two (or more) portfolios, each of which is overseen by a central agency.
- **Decentralized.** Intended to capture instances of significant fragmentation of SOE oversight, this model includes situations where SOEs are overseen without whole-of-government or centralized oversight, generally by line or sector ministries.

The Organisation for Economic Co-operation and Development (OECD) guidelines call for the centralization of the state's ownership function, as this can help avoid conflicts of interest by separating issues of ownership from other government functions that may impact SOEs. The majority of countries in a recent OECD survey have adopted a centralized model (footnote a). Many countries that have a central ministry coordinating most SOE ownership functions place this power under the Ministry of Finance (MoF) or equivalent institution.

Indonesia's Ministry of State-Owned Enterprises is unique when compared to peer countries, as SOEs in other Asian countries tend to be overseen either through their MoF, line or sector ministries, or an independent holding company rather than an SOE ministry.[b] Indonesia's system may be viewed as having previously had strong parallels with those countries that place SOE oversight under the MoF such as Thailand, where a State Enterprise Policy Office under the MoF exercises ownership rights. The SOE ownership model in Indonesia, given its characteristics and continued fragmentation, can best be classified as a "dual-ownership" model.

[a] OECD. 2018. *Ownership and Governance of SOEs: A Compendium of National Practices.* Paris.

[b] Asian Development Bank Institute. 2020. *Enhancing the Transparency and Accountability of SOEs.* Tokyo.

Source: Asian Development Bank.

18.   **The influence of other government entities.** SOEs, in their role as commercial entities and as development agents, are regulated and impacted by many other ministries. A list of the sector ministries impacting SOEs by current MSOE sector clusters can be viewed in the Appendix 1. Line and technical ministries set rates and prices that impact the viability of SOEs engaged in the provision of public goods, such as electricity, fuel, and fertilizers. Coordinating ministries, in their planning and coordination roles, also impact SOE operations. For instance, the Ministry of Energy and Mineral Resources has sole authority for setting electricity tariffs, even though MSOE oversees the sole electricity provider (PLN). Other quotas and subsidies such as liquefied petroleum gas and diesel prices are also set by sector ministries. Beyond the ministries, Parliament also exercises oversight authority, particularly for large SOEs. Apart from regulatory and oversight concerns, SOEs are also subject to political influence given the government's ownership role. Stakeholders mentioned instances of international investors appealing directly to government or elected officials to influence SOE behavior, illustrating the uniquely difficult position SOEs occupy within the economy as commercial institutions with strong ties to the state.

19.   **Ministry of State-Owned Enterprises' deep span of control and capacity constraints.** Beyond the complications introduced by multiple centers of control in SOE governance, the MSOE also takes a more active role in managing its holdings than advised under best practices, which recommend allowing SOEs independence. SOEs must seek authorization from the MSOE to carry out many investments, issue bonds, change their organization structure, establish subsidiaries, implement new human resource systems, or change their company logos, among other actions (Appendix 5). The thresholds requiring ministerial authorization depend on SOE size, setting lower thresholds for smaller SOEs. Staffing of SOE leadership is controlled by the MSOE, though systematization of the staffing process is lacking, and the MSOE is mandated to co-create business plans, budgets, and represent the government at shareholder meetings for each SOE. Many stakeholders felt that the MSOE is increasing its interventions into the operation of SOEs. The optics of scandals at SOEs, the direct financial cost, and potential legal penalties associated with losses of state assets have in part contributed to the adoption of such a deep span of control by the MSOE. Interventions into SOE business planning may lessen the quality of planning due to the MSOE's lack of responsibility for implementation and the absence of executives with relevant knowledge of the firm and sector. Such interventions create difficulties when the MSOE must later hold SOE boards accountable for plans those boards did not develop. International experience has highlighted the counterintuitive nature of the impact of state interventions, wherein more intrusions weaken governance and performance while increasing vulnerability to corruption (footnote 12).

20.   **Staffing limitations within the Ministry of State-Owned Enterprises.** This interventionism is in tension with the limited capacity and capability of the MSOE, as staff often do not possess the necessary skills or experience to produce or audit business plans for the commercial entities they oversee, and conflicts with best practices. The MSOE itself has 385 employees (as of 2020), who are tasked with overseeing over 100 SOEs (comprising a total of more than 1,000 entities when counting subsidiaries) with a total of 800,000 employees, more than $500 billion in assets (56.2% of Indonesian GDP as of 2019), and accounting for roughly 6% of Indonesian output (as of the most recent estimate in 2017).[31] MSOE employees tend to come from a bureaucratic background rather than from the private sector, and often lack the skills needed to evaluate commercial enterprises. Less than 25% of MSOE staff possess a master's degree equivalent or higher, while slightly more than 25% of MSOE staff have less than a bachelor's degree equivalent.[32] In contrast, Temasek, Singapore's successful SOE holding company, has fewer assets under management ($214 billion) and more employees (roughly 800), highlighting the capacity constraints under which the MSOE operates.[33] Until 2018, over 80% of MSOE staff were officially employees of the MoF and not the MSOE, which created poor incentives for MSOE to invest in its staff. A reform in 2018 transferred most of these employees from the MoF to the MSOE, which should better align incentives to support upskilling and training programs within the MSOE. Staffing has improved recently, along with a new ministry structure and the appointment of more officials with private sector experience (para. 41). Stakeholders estimated that the MSOE may require an additional 100–200 employees to fulfill its mission, and increasing the capability of its staff and the alignment of staff capabilities with the MSOE's governance mission must also be a priority.

---

[31]   Calculations based on MSOE data; E. Ginting and K. Naqvi, eds. 2020. *Reforms, Opportunities, and Challenges for State-Owned Enterprises.* Manila: ADB.

[32]   MSOE internal data.

[33]   Temasek. Who We Are: About Us.

B. Overview of the Role and Prominence of State-Owned Enterprises in the Indonesian Economy

21.   **Evolution of state-owned enterprises in the economy.** The Constitution of Indonesia mandates a role for the state in key sectors, explicitly calling for state control of "sectors of production which are important for the country and affect the life of the people."[34] During the Soekarno and Suharto eras, from independence to 1998, the government founded SOEs in several sectors and many foreign firms were nationalized, resulting in a wide variety of SOEs across sectors including shipping, agriculture, oil and gas, steel, chemicals, transportation, and communications, among others. While SOEs continue to operate in many of these sectors today, the size of SOEs relative to the economy and the contribution of SOEs to output have fallen. SOE assets as a share of GDP declined from the late 1980s until 2010, when this longstanding trend reversed (Figure 2). Since then, SOE assets have grown relative to the economy.[35] It is estimated that SOEs accounted for 6% of Indonesian GDP in 2017, a decline from an estimated 13% of total output in 1989 and a smaller share of total output than for other major emerging markets in the region.[36]

Figure 2: State-Owned Enterprises Assets as a Share of Indonesia's Gross Domestic Product

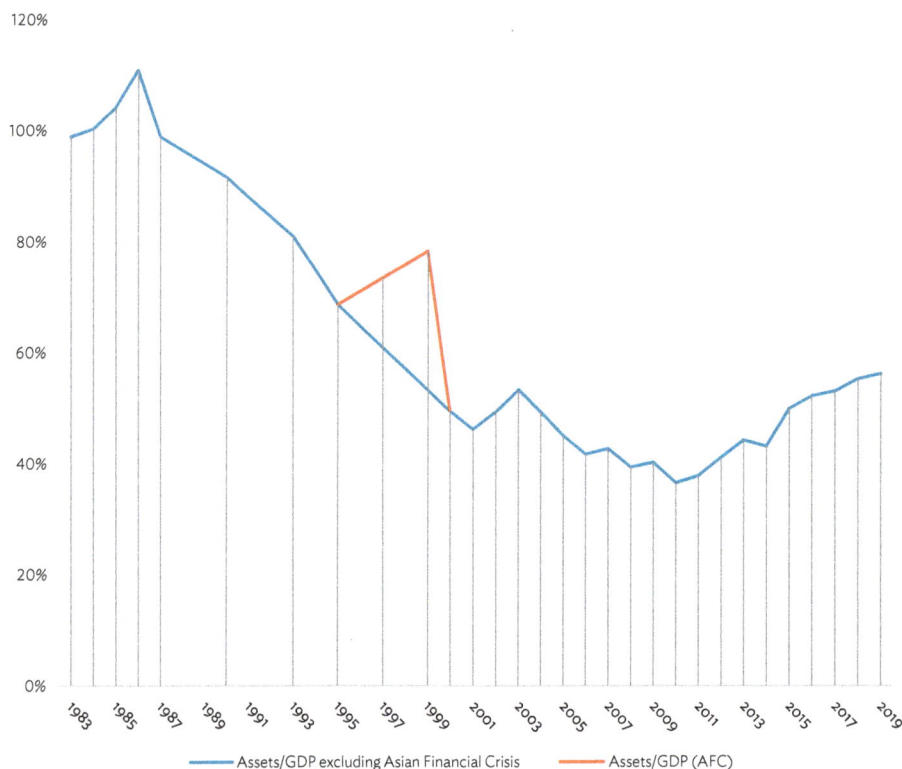

AFC = Asian financial crisis, GDP = gross domestic product, SOE = state-owned enterprise.

Source: Asian Development Bank calculations using data from the Ministry of State-Owned Enterprises and Statistics Indonesia (BPS).

---

34   Government of Indonesia. 1945. Constitution. Jakarta.
35   ADB. 2020. *Country Partnership Strategy: Indonesia, 2020–2024—Emerging Stronger.* Inclusive and Sustainable Growth Assessment (accessible from the list of linked documents in Appendix 3). Manila.
36   World Bank. 1995. *Bureaucrats in Business: The Economics and Politics of Government Ownership.* Washington, DC.

Table 1: State-Owned Enterprise Assets Show High Degree of Concentration

	Top 5	Top 10	Bottom 100	Bottom 75	Bottom 50
SOE assets by size, % of total SOE assets (2019)	68.6	80.9	12.1	2.3	0.5

SOE = state-owned enterprise.

Note: There were a total of 114 SOEs in 2019.

Source: Asian Development Bank calculations using SOE data from the Ministry of State-Owned Enterprises (accessed in 2020).

22.   **Overview of current state-owned enterprises.** As of 2019, the 10 largest SOEs overseen by MSOE in terms of assets included those in energy (Pertamina, PLN), banking (Bank Mandiri, Bank Negara Indonesia, Bank Rakyat Indonesia, and Bank Tabungan Negara), pension funds (PT Taspen), telecommunications (Telkom), mining (Mining Industry Indonesia), and fertilizer (PT Pupuk). Together, these 10 SOEs accounted for more than 80% of SOE assets in 2019 (Table 1). Several other large SOEs are involved in infrastructure construction and operation, and the infrastructure SOEs have seen particularly rapid growth in terms of assets with assets of all infrastructure SOEs up 833% over the 2010–2019 period, the fastest growth in assets for a sector (a further discussion of the large infrastructure SOEs is in Box 2). Other large SOEs include those in agriculture (PT Perkebunan Nusantara III), manufacturing (PT Krakatau Steel), logistics (several airport and port operators), and Indonesia's flag carrier (Garuda Indonesia). Smaller SOEs operate in sectors as varied as film production (Perum Produksi Film Negara), nuclear technology (PT Industri Nuklir Indonesia), hospitality (PT Hotel Indonesia Natour), and ferry operation (PT ASDP Indonesia Ferry). Small SOEs account for a very limited portion of SOE assets. The 75 smallest SOEs in terms of assets accounted for just 2.3% of total SOE assets, and the smallest 50 SOEs by this measure accounted for just 0.5% of total SOE assets.

23.   **State-owned enterprises as agents of development.** In line with their constitutionally mandated purpose, SOEs in Indonesia are often used by the government to support policy goals. Throughout ADB's consultation with the MSOE and SOE leadership, stakeholders frequently emphasized the role of SOEs in correcting market failures, often highlighting how Indonesia's archipelagic geography and varying levels of development contribute to a heightened potential for market failure and necessitate a role for state intervention in the corporate sector through SOEs. SOEs can be mandated to provide goods to the public at certain prices (most notably in the cases of fuel and fertilizer), be assigned to build infrastructure, or be mandated to provide services (such as financial or telecommunications) where private firms may not be willing to due to viability concerns. SOEs carrying out such PSOs are generally compensated by the government (para. 34). In recent years, the use of SOEs as agents of development has been particularly prominent in the case of infrastructure, with SOEs currently providing one-third of infrastructure investment.[37] SOEs can play an important role in helping Indonesia achieve its climate goals (Box 3). However, SOEs may not be the most efficient means through which to achieve some policy goals, as SOEs may create unnecessary distortions in the economy and generate hidden costs.

24.   **Public listings.** Many of the largest SOEs in Indonesia are publicly listed companies. Partial privatizations through stock listings have resulted in SOEs accounting for more than half of SOE assets being publicly traded to some degree (Figure 3). While there was a large push toward privatization following the Asian financial crisis, "privatization" of Indonesian SOEs largely took the form of partial listings of SOEs rather than full government divestment (Appendix 2 has a list of privatization actions by year). Cases of full state divestment were largely limited to the holdings of the Indonesian Bank Restructuring Agency (IBRA), which divested state holdings in several commercial banks acquired during the Asian financial crisis.[38] The state also fully divested its minority shares in several firms but only gave up its majority share of one SOE, Indosat, which now operates as a private firm.

[37]   E. Ginting and K. Naqvi, eds. 2020. *Reforms, Opportunities, and Challenges for State-Owned Enterprises.* Manila: ADB.
[38]   Y. Sato. 2004. Bank Restructuring and Financial Institution Reform in Indonesia. *The Developing Economies.* 43 (1). pp. 91–120.

Box 2: Infrastructure State-Owned Enterprises Case Study

A major shift within the state-owned enterprises (SOEs) sector since 2014 has been the rapid growth of SOEs involved in the provision of infrastructure, particularly Waskita Karya, Adhi Karya, Wijaya Karya, Hutama Karya, and PTPP. These are considered the key infrastructure SOEs. A key priority of President Joko Widodo has been the increased provision of infrastructure, due to the Government of Indonesia's identification of a large infrastructure gap as a constraint on Indonesia's growth. However, the government is limited in the amount it can spend due to its low receipts (government revenue as a share of gross domestic product [GDP] averaged just 12.7% of GDP from 2015–2019) and a statutory limit on the government deficit of 3% of GDP.[a] To encourage construction while staying within the government's fiscal deficit ceiling, SOEs were asked to take on large projects. In addition to the budget constraint incentivizing government reliance on SOEs, SOEs have also been attractive due to direct government influence over SOE operations and easy access to financing due to perceived sovereign backing.

Infrastructure State-Owned Enterprise Growth and Performance

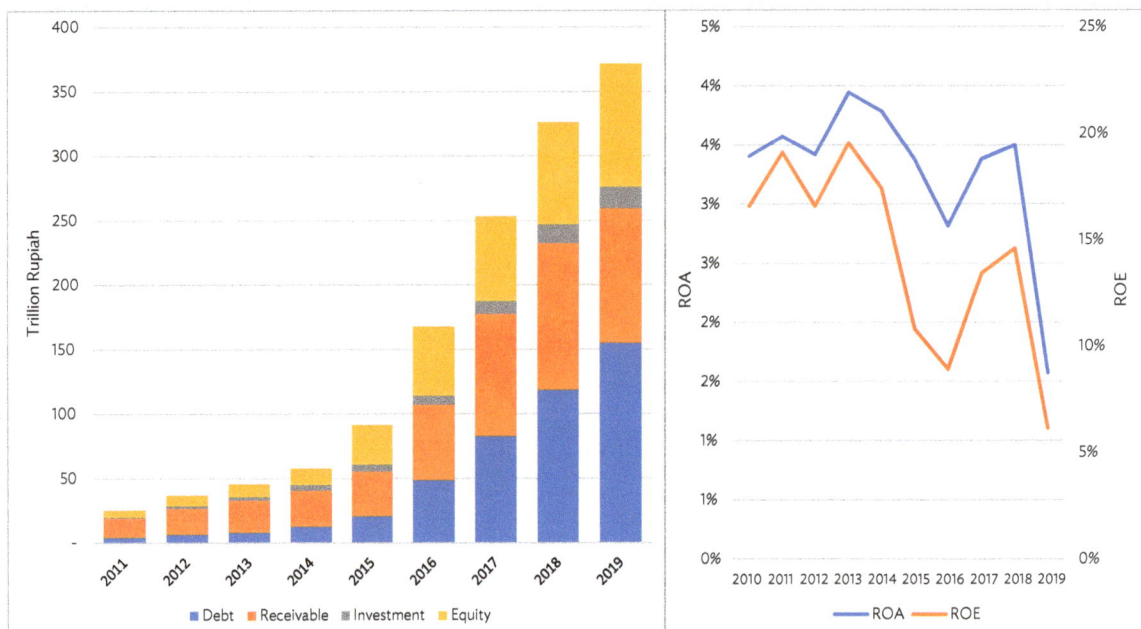

ROA = return on asset, ROE = return on equity.

Source: Asian Development Bank calculations using data from the Ministry of State-Owned Enterprises.

Prior to 2014, these key infrastructure SOEs were more involved in smaller-scale building construction than in infrastructure megaprojects, but since then they have been tasked with carrying out the government's infrastructure investment policy aims. To increase the capacity of SOEs to provide infrastructure, the five largest construction SOEs were given Rp8.5 trillion in equity injections in 2014, an additional Rp8.2 trillion in 2015, and Rp10.5 trillion in 2019. The total assets of these five SOEs totaled Rp59.5 trillion in 2014, and by 2019 had ballooned to Rp372.0 trillion (about $26.4 billion equivalent) for an average annual growth rate of 44% over 5 years. This growth has seen SOEs become prominent providers of infrastructure.[b] Rapid growth has brought with it stresses. The rate at which the firms complete their projects has slowed, meaning that it takes them longer to convert working capital into cash. This has led to these firms taking on further debt to support their working capital investments (see figure).

[a] ADB. 2020. *Country Partnership Strategy: Indonesia, 2020–2024—Emerging Stronger*. Inclusive and Sustainable Growth Assessment (accessible from the list of linked documents in Appendix 3). Manila.

[b] World Bank. Infrastructure Sector Assessment. Jakarta. Unpublished.

Source: Asian Development Bank

Box 3: Climate and State-Owned Enterprises

Indonesia will both be heavily affected by climate change and, as a large developing economy, will necessarily play a central part in global efforts to limit it. State-owned enterprises (SOEs), similarly, will be impacted by climate change and can be a key tool for addressing climate change and environmental degradation. State involvement in the private sector can be best justified by the need to correct market failures, which loom particularly large when considering climate issues, making coordinated policy through SOEs a possible avenue for correcting climate-related market failures.

SOEs, particularly energy producers and the State Electricity Company (PLN) but also SOEs in other sectors, have the potential to play a role in driving Indonesia's transition by setting higher standards for energy efficiency and lowering their emissions. Pertamina, as a producer of fossil fuels, can be a leader in transitioning to greener alternatives. PLN's emissions are projected to total 264 million tons of carbon dioxide in 2021, with projected future growth climbing to 461 tons annually by 2030 under business as usual, or to 349 tons under PLN's most optimistic low carbon intensity projection. Indonesia's growing energy needs will likely require greater production of energy, and PLN can be a key driver of a transition to greener production, as anticipated under its plan to achieve carbon neutrality by 2050.[a] One recent initiative is a move toward mandating the use of biodiesel, and other green initiatives are planned. Geo Dipa, an SOE currently under the Ministry of Finance, is a leader in geothermal energy in Indonesia. Further consolidation of state-owned geothermal companies could support the development of additional potential renewable energy sources.[b] Financial SOEs can also assess the climate impact of their investments and clients while developing green financial products.

Several SOEs in the agriculture sector manage large areas of Indonesia's forests. Perum Perhutani, the state forestry holding company, manages 2.4 million hectares of Indonesian forest in Java and Madura, accounting for 2% of Indonesia's total forested area. Perum Perhutani has taken a relatively hands-off management style, engaging with contractors for limited logging, and has not been a major presence in the forestry sector despite its large holdings. Ensuring the health and good management of these forests can provide Indonesia with a carbon sink, which could potentially be a new business model for managing these forests.

It is important to note that SOEs may also negatively impact Indonesia's climate goals. Inefficient production, a lack of abidance with climate regulations (observed in other contexts), and difficulties transitioning to greener power can all pose problems. In order to ensure SOEs help support a transition to cleaner energy rather than act as an impediment to such a transition, clear goals should be communicated with effective benchmarking for climate targets and environmental, social, and governance targets should be set.

PLN = Perusahaan Listrik Negara.

[a] D. F. Rahman. 2021. PLN Pledges Carbon Neutrality by 2050. *The Jakarta Post*. 8 May.

[b] A. Richter. 2021. Plans on Merging State-Owned Geothermal Companies in Indonesia Back on the Table. *Think GeoEnergy*. 7 February.

Source: Asian Development Bank.

Figure 3: Publicly Traded State-Owned Enterprises as Share of State-Owned Enterprises Assets

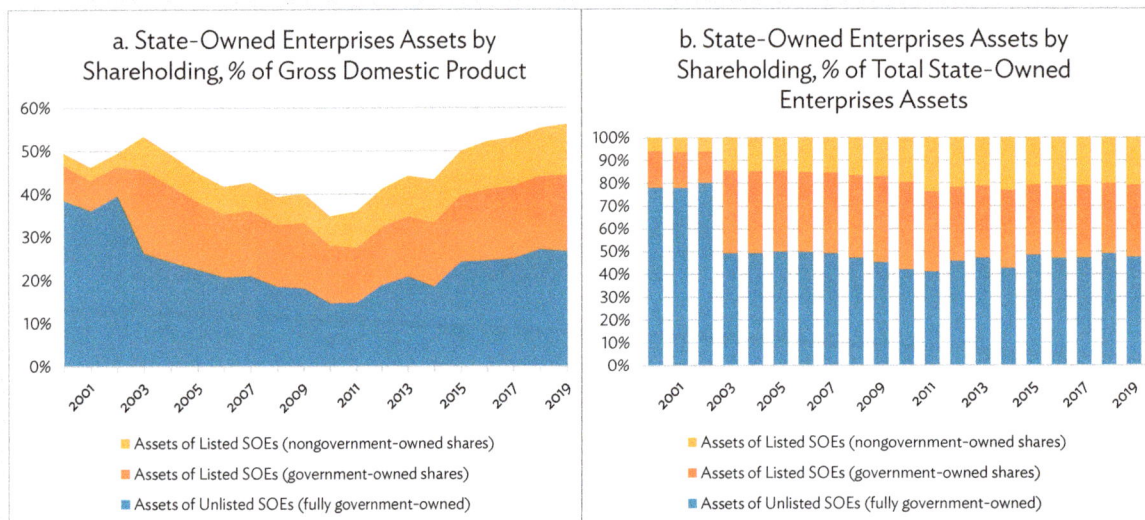

SOE = state-owned enterprise.

Source: Asian Development Bank calculations using data from the Ministry of State-Owned Enterprises and Statistics Indonesia (BPS).

25.   **The political economy of privatization.** The lack of many full divestments contrasts with government commitments to the International Monetary Fund (IMF) to pursue full privatization following the Asian financial crisis and ADB support for SOE privatizations over this period.[39] Most major partial privatizations occurred prior to 2003, when several large financial SOEs had initial public offerings (IPOs). The slowdown in privatizations may be attributable to the requirements of the SOE Law in 2003, which set a new requirement of parliamentary consent for privatizations (para. 10), combined with a general political climate opposed to privatization. The MSOE continued to make repeated commitments to privatizations until its 2010–2014 master plan, but more privatizations were planned than were executed, and privatization was not a key component of the subsequent 2015–2019 master plan.[40] Resistance to privatization stems from political economy concerns, with privatization commonly perceived as a transfer of state assets to foreign ownership.[41] Recent changes to the Privatization Committee (para. 10) as of March 2021 have signaled a potential willingness to consider pursuing limited divestments.[42]

---

[39] ADB. 2008. *Completion Report: State-Owned Enterprise Governance and Privatization Program in Indonesia.* Manila; IMF. 1998. Indonesia Letter of Intent, 13 November 1998. Jakarta.

[40] *Privatisasi* (privatization) is mentioned 164 times in the 2010–2014 roadmap, and once in the 2015–2019 roadmap. Government of Indonesia, MSOE. 2010. *Master Plan Badan Usaha Milik Negara 2010–2014 (SOE Master Plan 2010–2014).* Jakarta; Government of Indonesia, MSOE. 2010. *Roadmap BUMN 2015–2019.* Jakarta.

[41] T. Praseniantono. 2004. Political Economy of Privatisation of State-Owned Enterprises in Indonesia. In M. C. Basri and P. v. d. Eng, eds. *Business in Indonesia: New Challenges, Old Problems.* ISEAS-Yusof Ishak Institute. Singapore; ADB. 2009. *Validation Report: State-Owned Enterprise Governance and Privatization Program in Indonesia (Independent Evaluation Department).* Manila.

[42] Government of Indonesia. 2021. Keputusan Presiden (KEPPRES) 2/2021 (Amendment to Presidential Decree Number 47 of 2014 concerning the Public Company [Persero] Privatization Committee). Jakarta.

26.   **Consolidation of state-owned enterprises.** The reduction in the number of SOEs from 141 in 2010 to 114 in 2019 and 104 as of early 2021 has been achieved through the consolidation of SOEs. Figure 4 provides an example, with PT Inhutani I–V, SOEs operating in the forestry sector, being consolidated under Perum Perhutani in 2013. Other consolidations have included those of fertilizer firms under Pupuk and cement producers under Semen Indonesia (in 2012), the plantation firms Perkebunan Nusantara I–II and IV–XIV under Perkebunan Nusantara III (completed in 2014), several mining firms under Mining Industry Indonesia (2017), consolidating Perusahaan Gas Negara under Pertamina (2018), and consolidation of the state pharmaceuticals firms under Biofarma and state hospitals under the Indonesia Healthcare Corporation. The consolidation of SOEs will need to continue focusing on increasing the viability of the firms along with the reduction in the headline number of SOEs. The restructuring process should refrain from creating additional subsidiaries, which may weaken the application of the SOE Law to these entities in the future.

Figure 4: Example of State-Owned Enterprise Consolidation

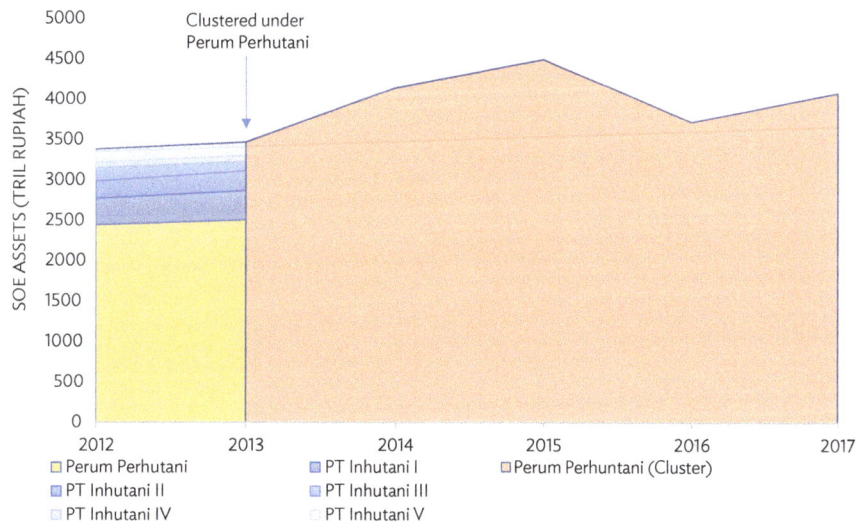

Rp = rupiah, SOEs = state-owned enterprises.

Source: Asian Development Bank calculations using data from the Ministry of State-Owned Enterprises.

III. Assessing the Performance of State-Owned Enterprises: Economic and Social Value

27.   The performance of SOEs in both their economic and social contribution to Indonesia is mixed. Some SOEs are among the most competitive firms in Indonesia, including dynamic, technologically advanced firms (Box 4), while other SOEs perform poorly. Assessing the efficiency and profitability of SOEs is difficult, as many SOEs are required to provide PSOs and may be better thought of as development-focused entities rather than as commercial firms (footnote 37). However, as appropriate PSO compensation structures should limit or eliminate the adverse impact of PSOs on SOEs and many SOEs primarily act as commercial entities, assessing measures of performance can help identify potential troubles with PSO compensation or commercial viability.

Box 4: State-Owned Enterprises and Technology

Indonesia's state-owned enterprises (SOEs) include dynamic, technologically advanced firms, which have the potential to act as drivers of Indonesia's technological transformation. SOEs and the Ministry of State-Owned Enterprises, have launched several programs to encourage adoption of more advanced technologies and practices.

- Firms such as Telkom are among Indonesia's most productive, and have helped to support the development of other innovative firms. Telkom's MDI Ventures, an innovative venture capital firm focused on supporting technology start-ups, aims to help create an innovation economy in Indonesia.[a] Notably, MDI Ventures has been able to balance the demands of state ownership with the risks inherent to venture capital, and can set an example for increased state support for innovative, cutting-edge firms.
- Pertamina has launched a digital payments interface, MyPertamina, which now has over 7 million registered users.[b] Digital systems like this one can help increase the data available to SOEs, better enabling them to develop new products and better target products to consumers. Better data can also aid SOEs in fulfilling their roles as providers of social value while improving the ability of SOEs to target subsidies.
- SOEs can help spur research and development in Indonesia. Many of Indonesia's large SOEs operate educational partnerships with institutes of higher education in Indonesia. An Asian Development Bank report recommends that SOEs foster collaboration with institutes of higher education for research and training programs, which can establish a supporting environment for technological advancement in Indonesia.[c]
- Indonesia Digital Healthcare is a project aiming to integrate hospitals (to be overseen by the future Indonesia Healthcare Corporation, which is currently under development), SOE clinics, and pharmacies, along with payment systems from SOE banks. The creation of a more integrated healthcare system can help deliver better service to consumers.
- During the coronavirus disease pandemic, SOEs have played a key role in developing technological solutions to aid vaccine distribution throughout Indonesia. Applications developed by Telkom, integrated with the distribution systems of Indonesia's pharmaceutical SOEs, have helped aid Indonesia's vaccine delivery efforts.

[a] MDI. About Us.
[b] Pertamina. MyPertamina.
[c] Asian Development Bank. 2020. *Innovate Indonesia: Unlocking Growth through Technological Transformation*. Manila.

Source: Asian Development Bank.

28.   **SOEs face a variety of constraints to their performance.** Even within commercially focused SOEs, SOEs tend to be more bureaucratic than private firms and have fewer market incentives than private firms (though past reforms have increased the number of publicly traded SOEs). They also face a variety of challenges resulting from a lack of management stability, long-term planning, and incentives or ability to pursue necessary internal reforms to improve their performance, as well as their limited scope for independent decision-making.[43] While the developmental role of SOEs is also prominent, many SOEs require clearer rationale for state ownership and the government's use of SOEs to achieve policy aims has sometimes been costly and inefficient, and may have large hidden costs. This section provides an overview and assessment of SOE commercial performance in Part A, followed by an evaluation of the performance of SOEs as non-commercial entities and the impact of PSOs in Part B. Both of these subsections primarily focus on the pre-COVID-19 pandemic period; the use of SOEs during the pandemic are discussed in Section IV.

29.   **State-owned enterprises performance varies significantly.** Historically, many SOEs have struggled to maintain commercial viability and financial health. A 1989 review by the MoF found that 66% of SOEs were "unhealthy" based on their financial indicators.[44] Adopting a framework similar to a recent ADB report on Indonesian SOEs, 43 of the 114 SOEs as of 2019 failed to meet low thresholds for financial viability (achieving at least half of the sector average return on equity [ROE] for emerging market firms; Appendix 3 has more details). However, the listed SOEs on the Indonesia Stock Exchange (IDX) tend to outperform the overall ROE of IDX-listed firms (Figure 5a). The performance of SOEs is characterized by a divergence between a few strong performers, which are generally large SOEs, and a large number of smaller poor performers.[45] Commercially unviable SOEs tend to be small, with the overall assets of the 43 unviable SOEs identified by our criteria accounting for roughly one-quarter of total SOE assets, and the majority of assets held by unviable SOEs are held by electricity utility PLN (Figure 5b). Unviable SOEs are spread across many sectors, but roughly a third are involved in manufacturing, including firms like steel producer Krakatau Steel and glass producer Iglas (Appendix 3 provides further analysis of manufacturing SOE performance based on the Large and Medium-Scale Manufacturing Survey). Other sectors with substantial numbers of unviable SOEs include logistics (such as toll operator Indra Karya) and food and agriculture (including the holding company PT Rajawali Nusantara Indonesia [RNI] and fisheries operator PT Perikanan Nusantara). Given the difficulty of closing down SOEs, which requires parliamentary approval and support from the Privatization Committee, SOEs are effectively not subject to solvency proceedings and poorly performing SOEs are not closed down even when such a closure would be appropriate.

[43]   M. Indreswari. 2006. Corporate Governance of Indonesian State-Owned Enterprises. Thesis presented for the degree of Doctor Philosophy in Development Studies at Massey University, Palmerston North, New Zealand.

[44]   Sjahrir. 1990. The Indonesian Economy Facing the 1990s. *Southeast Asian Affairs*. pp. 117–131.

[45]   M. E. Rayess et al. 2019. Indonesia's Public Wealth: A Balance Sheet Approach to Fiscal Policy Analysis. *IMF Working Paper*. No. 19/81. 24 April. Washington, DC.

**Figure 5: Listed State-Owned Enterprise Performance
and State-Owned Enterprise Viability by Size**

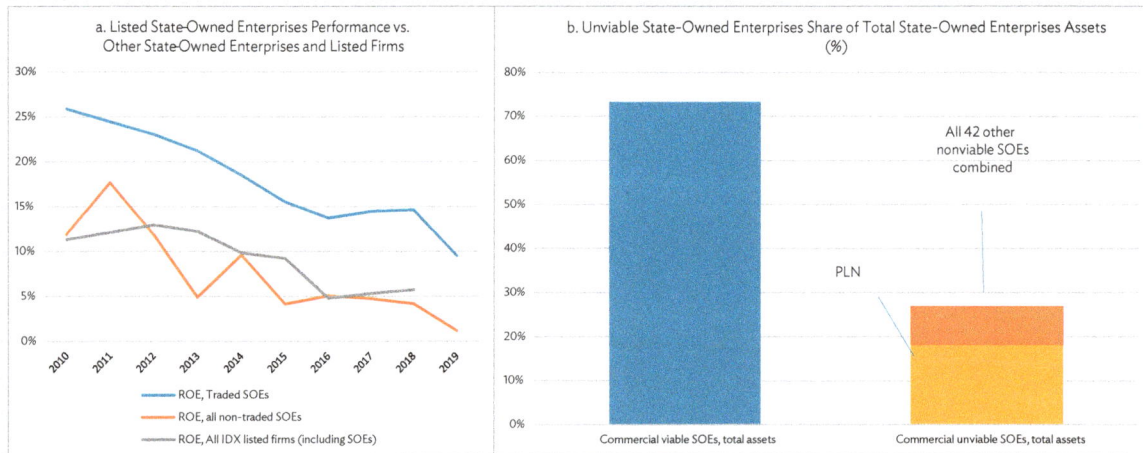

IDX = Indonesia Stock Exchange, PLN = Perusahaan Listrik Negara, ROE = return on equity, SOE = state-owned enterprise.

Source: Asian Development Bank calculations using data from the Ministry of State-Owned Enterprises, Statistics Indonesia (BPS), and Indonesia Stock Exchange.

A. State-Owned Enterprises as Commercial Entities: Performers and Problems

30.   **Indonesian state-owned enterprise performance in context.** Figure 6 compares the performance of Indonesian SOEs with the average sector-level ROE across all emerging markets during 2015–2019.[46] The sectors in Figure 6 are the 10 sectors with the greatest value of Indonesian SOE assets in 2019, comprised of 49 SOEs accounting for 94.7% of total SOE assets in 2019. The ROE of Indonesian SOEs exceeds the emerging market average in telecommunications services, the shipbuilding and maritime sector, metals and mining, and construction, and is roughly the emerging market average in banking. In the other five sectors, the ROE of Indonesian SOEs is below the emerging market average. Many of the sectors with lower ROE than the emerging market average are ones where SOEs provide public goods and services (oil and gas and power). As such, ROE may not be the most appropriate metric to assess these firms (more discussion of the developmental role of SOEs is provided in part B of this section). ROE is notably far below average in the insurance sector, due to recent large losses linked to two state insurers (para. 32). Performance does not appear to be linked to the degree of competition in a particular industry, with varying levels of performance in sectors with a high and low degree of competition.

---

[46]   Sector definitions as in Damodaran Online. Data: Current and Data: Archives. Accessed January 2021. See Annex 3 for additional details on data construction.

Figure 6: Return on Equity of State-Owned Enterprises in Indonesia in International Context

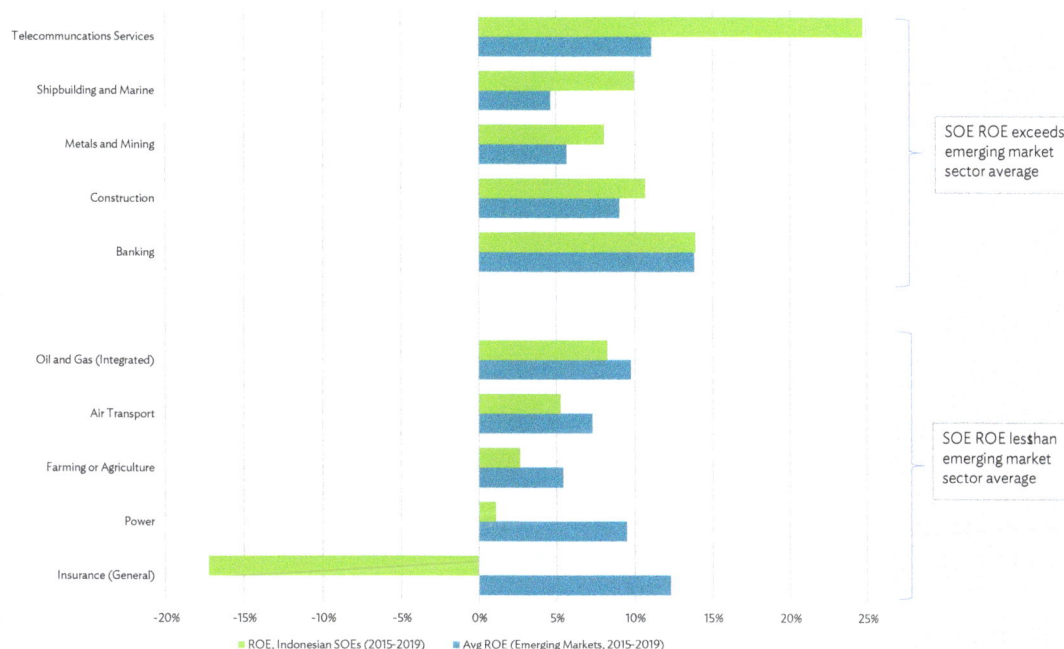

ROE = return on equity, SOE = state-owned enterprise.

Source: Asian Development Bank calculations using data from the Ministry of State-Owned Enterprises and Damodaran Online. Data: Current and Data: Archives. Accessed January 2021.

31.   **Publicly listing state-owned enterprises may improve performance.** Publicly listed SOEs in Indonesia often perform better than other SOEs (para. 29). While there is a clear link between strong SOE performance and the suitability of public listing, a positive and significant performance boost resulting from (even partial) privatization has been identified across several international studies.[47] MSOE data from 2000–2019, a period that covers most listings of SOEs, allows an assessment of the impact of public listings on SOE performance in Indonesia, particularly the relationship between the share of a company that is publicly traded and its subsequent performance in terms of return on assets (ROA) and ROE (more details on the data and construction of our measures are in Appendix 3). Table 2 evaluates two models of how listing may impact performance. In the first, the relationship between SOE performance and the percentage of its shares that are publicly traded does not depend on firm size (columns 1–2 and 5–6, without an interaction term) and in the second, the relationship does depend on firm size (columns 3–4 and 7–8, with an interaction term). The results find a robust positive relationship between the listed share of a firm and subsequent firm performance as measured by both ROA and ROE in most specifications. This relationship is particularly robust in specifications where the impact of privatization is allowed to vary with firm size, suggesting that for larger firms, there is a stronger relationship between publicly traded shares and firm performance (these specifications are discussed in more detail in Appendix 3). While this analysis cannot establish a causal relationship, consultations with the corporate leadership of several publicly traded SOEs highlighted the many potential channels through which

---

[47]   S. Estrin and A. Pelletier. 2018. Privatization in Developing Countries: What Are the Lessons of Recent Experience. *World Bank Research Observer.* 33 (1). pp. 65–102. Washington, DC.

nongovernment shareholding may help improve SOE performance. Nongovernment shareholders often insist on better corporate practices, push for long-term planning, and provide SOEs with more leverage to negotiate PSOs. Public listing also has immediate benefits for SOE governance and transparency, given the higher reporting requirements placed on listed firms.[48] While the available evidence does not establish causality, the results are consistent with public listing playing a role in improving SOE performance.

Table 2: Public Listing and State-Owned Enterprise Performance

	ROA				ROE			
	(1)	(2)	(3)	(4)	(5)	(6)	(7)	(8)
% Traded (prior)	0.119***	0.0130	0.214***	0.163***	0.161***	0.00934	0.329***	0.209**
	(0.0193)	(0.0281)	(0.0585)	(0.0522)	(0.0181)	(0.0456)	(0.0612)	(0.0914)
Ln(Assets, % GDP)	−0.00768***	−0.00284	−0.00874***	−0.000450	0.00282	−0.0161	0.000843	−0.0135
	(0.00161)	(0.00915)	(0.00183)	(0.00860)	(0.00232)	(0.0126)	(0.00276)	(0.0121)
% Traded (prior) X			0.0181*	0.0278**			0.0320***	0.0369**
Ln(Assets, % GDP)			(0.0106)	(0.0109)			(0.0104)	(0.0126)
Year FE	Yes	Yes	Yes	Yes	Yes	Yes	Yes	Yes
Firm FE		Yes		Yes		Yes		Yes
Std. Error Cluster		Yes (firm)		Yes (firm)		Yes (firm)		Yes (firm)
Adj. R2	0.087	0.683	0.088	0.693	0.123	0.567	0.126	0.574
N	943	277	943	277	910	266	910	266

GDP = gross domestic product, ROA = return on asset, ROE = return on equity, SOE = state-owned enterprise, FE = fixed effect.

Notes:

1. Standard errors in parentheses, * $p<0.10$, ** $p<0.05$, *** $p<0.01$.
2. The sample consists of the 50 largest SOEs (by assets) in 2019, from 2000 to 2019 (see appendix for robustness checks).
3. In Columns 2, 4, 6, and 8 standard errors are clustered by firm and the sample includes only firms with nongovernment shareholding from 2000–2019.

Source: Asian Development Bank calculations using data from the Ministry of State-Owned Enterprises.

32.   **Operational and financial mismanagement.** Poor management and lax governance of SOEs, particularly before democratization, was acknowledged to be the root cause of several failures and notable instances of corruption.[49] Recent scandals have also been linked to alleged mismanagement, such as collapses at state-owned insurers Jiwasraya and ASABRI. Jiwasraya failed to pay out Rp18 trillion in matured policies due in 2020, and it was revealed that the insurer had invested in junk stocks.[50] A Rp20 trillion state expenditure has been proposed for 2021 to settle claims of fraud at Jiwasraya, demonstrating the state's implicit guarantee of SOEs.[51] ASABRI, which manages pensions for the military and police, suffered a loss of Rp23 trillion potentially due to similar mismanagement and investment in junk stocks.[52] With investigations ongoing, it appears these costly incidents are linked both to mismanagement and possible corruption. The costliness of such cases exemplifies why the state has become increasingly involved in the day–to–day management of SOEs and has defined strict punishments for "state losses." However, state intervention of this kind is unlikely to fully avoid these types of cases, and may have further negative effects on SOE dynamism. Preventing similar

---

[48]   IDX. 2004. Rule I-E Concerning the Obligation of Information Submission. Jakarta.

[49]   In 1975, Pertamina crashed due to mismanagement, its debts equivalent to roughly 30% of the GDP. H. Hill. 2000. Indonesia: The Strange and Sudden Death of a Tiger Economy. *Oxford Development Studies*. 28 (2). pp. 117–139.

[50]   G. Gumelar. 2020. Jiwasraya: Understanding Indonesia's Largest Financial Scandal. *The Jakarta Post*. 26 October. Jakarta.

[51]   A. W. Akhlas. 2020. SOEs to Receive Rp 40t Injection in 2021, Support Economic Recovery. *The Jakarta Post*. 9 November. Jakarta.

[52]   R. Rahman. 2020. Two Directors Lose Jobs over Investment Losses at State-Owned Asabri. *The Jakarta Post*. 30 January. Jakarta.

mismanagement in the future will require SOEs to adopt better governance practices. These will help ensure that SOEs are transparent, maintain professional boards, and have a high level of accountability.[53]

33.   **Staffing limitations.** Possible mismanagement is the result of many factors, but one contributing factor is the staffing practices of SOEs and the limitations that SOEs face. Stakeholders emphasized that they felt SOEs often struggled to ensure they were well-staffed and had qualified people in management and board roles. SOEs must receive permission from the MSOE to create many positions and face strict salary caps, making it difficult to compete with the private sector for talent. Upper management, including boards, have historically been politically appointed (particularly at SOE subsidiaries, para. 13) and may not be qualified for their roles. These challenges have manifested in the rapid turnover among the management of many SOEs. New standards have since been set for remuneration, performance benchmarks, management of the appointment and dismissal of boards of directors and commissioners of SOEs, and the assessment of candidates for positions. These new standards may help encourage better practices.

B. State-Owned Enterprises as Noncommercial Entities: Costs and Achievements

34.   **Providing and paying for public service obligations.** Beyond their commercial aims, SOEs are also often called upon to provide public goods. Many SOEs regularly provide PSOs, with 12 SOEs receiving regular subsidies to compensate for PSOs and many others receiving equity injections to support PSO provision (particularly in the infrastructure sector). Further, many other SOEs that do not usually provide PSOs have been called upon during the COVID-19 pandemic to support public policy aims, such as the SOE commercial banks that have played a key role in distributing government funds, the SOE pharmaceutical companies that are aiding in vaccine distribution, and SOE tech firms that have helped develop technology to support distribution (para. 43). While the role of the government in providing many of the public goods achieved through SOE PSOs is critical, the use of SOEs has been criticized in some cases as inefficient. The targeting of subsidized goods by SOEs has often been poor, while the structure of subsidies may encourage inefficient production.[54] Further, the government's preferential use of SOEs for infrastructure provision disadvantages the private sector, and the use of equity injections to compensate SOEs has created financial stresses for these firms. Before assigning public service obligations, including national strategic projects, financing for them needs to be pre-approved by the MoF for fiscal commitment, the MSOE for the SOE's capacity to implement the projects, and the technical ministry on the project's technical specification.

35.   **Equity injections to state-owned enterprises.** Indonesia has tended to compensate PSOs for infrastructure through equity injections to SOEs, wherein the government provides an infusion of cash or assets. For the government budget, this structure has the advantage of requiring just one expenditure, which is generally less than the cost of the project as SOEs are expected to leverage the additional equity, shifting borrowing from the state to the SOE. This financing structure creates financial stresses for SOEs, as they must take on debt to (in some cases) execute commercially nonviable projects. This reliance on equity injections has also made it difficult for the private sector to participate in many projects because equity injections are not a viable means of compensating nonstate firms.[55] From 2010 to 2019, Rp126 trillion (about $8 billion equivalent) of equity injections were made to SOEs from the state budget (Figure 9b).[56] Considering this pre-COVID-19 crisis period during 2010–2019 in more detail (large expenditures on SOEs related to the COVID-19 pandemic are discussed further in para. 43),

[53]   OECD. 2018. *Guidelines on Anti-Corruption and Integrity in State-Owned Enterprises*. Paris.
[54]   World Bank. 2020. *Indonesia Public Expenditure Review 2020: Spending for Better Results*. Jakarta.
[55]   World Bank. Infrastructure Sector Assessment. Unpublished.
[56]   Data from MSOE; exchange rates were calculated on an annual basis using the average United States dollar to Indonesia rupiah exchange rate.

equity injections are generally a small portion of the overall budget. Exceptions were in 2015 and 2016 when equity injections were nearly 3% of the state budget. The 2015 injections went to 31 SOEs operating in several sectors; large sums were provided to SOEs involved in infrastructure provision and PLN (Box 5). Additional large injections in 2016 went to fewer firms (12 SOEs) with the majority of capital going to PLN. PLN thus received 31.6% of the value of equity injections from 2010–2019, totaling Rp40 trillion. A large share of the value of equity injections has also been directed toward the SOEs prominently involved in infrastructure provision, which received 24.2% of the total value of injections in 2010–2019 (Rp30.7 trillion in total).

Box 5: Perusahaan Listrik Negara Case Study

The case of Perusahaan Listrik Negara (State Electricity Company, or PLN) illustrates well the challenges of managing state intervention in the economy. PLN is one of the largest state-owned enterprises (SOEs) in Indonesia, with total assets of Rp1.5 quadrillion (roughly $114 billion, or 10% of Indonesian gross domestic product) in 2019. It is one of the largest utilities in the world, with a monopoly on electricity transmission and ownership of a majority of Indonesia's power generation capacity and nearly all transmission infrastructure.[a] PLN is reliant on government support due to a tariff structure that does not reflect the cost of supply and a government mandate to accelerate the development of the country's power generation capacity even in the absence of market demand. PLN's capacity to manage Indonesia's future energy transition will depend on significant government support and institutional reforms.

Government Support to PLN and Size of Subsidy

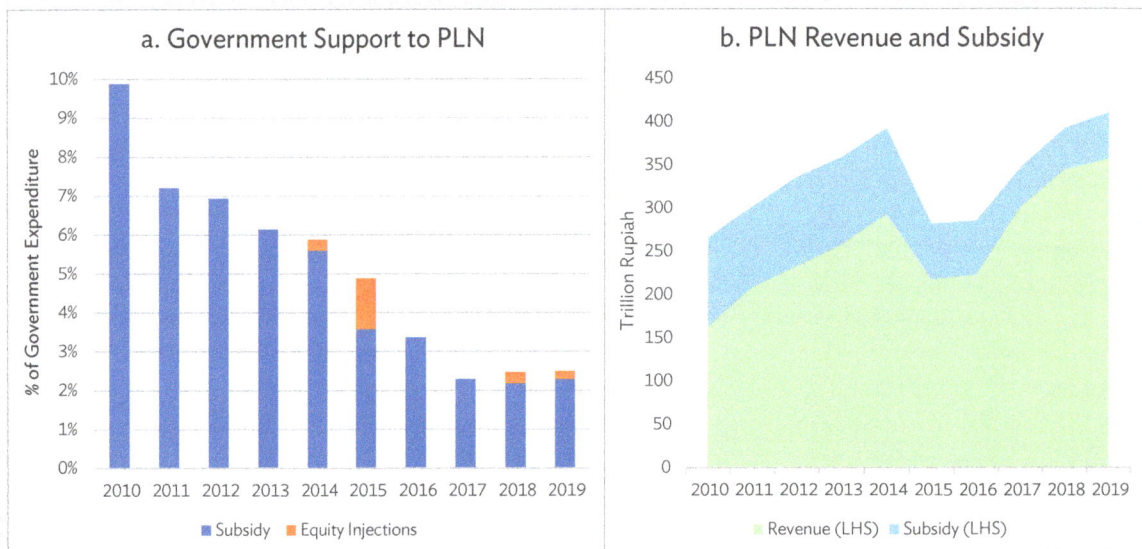

LHS = left-hand scale, PLN = Perusahaan Listrik Negara (State Electricity Company).

Source: Asian Development Bank calculations using data from the Ministry of State-Owned Enterprises.

PLN is subject to government mandates to provide electricity at less than the cost of production for which it is compensated through government subsidies covering PLN's cost margin plus 7%, a production subsidy structure that can encourage inefficient production (although recent guidance has tied payments to PLN performance). The total cost of this subsidy is currently 2% of government expenditures, down from roughly 10% of government expenditure in 2010 (see figure). However, the reform process that contributed to lessening the budget impact of the subsidy appears to have stalled as automatic rate adjustment mechanisms were suspended in 2018 and rate adjustments in 2020 further lowered electricity prices. The true extent of effective government subsidies may also be understated as other policies, such as a cap on the price of coal sold to PLN, distort the market prices of PLN's inputs.[b]

continued on next page

Box 5 *continued*

PLN Debt and Utilization

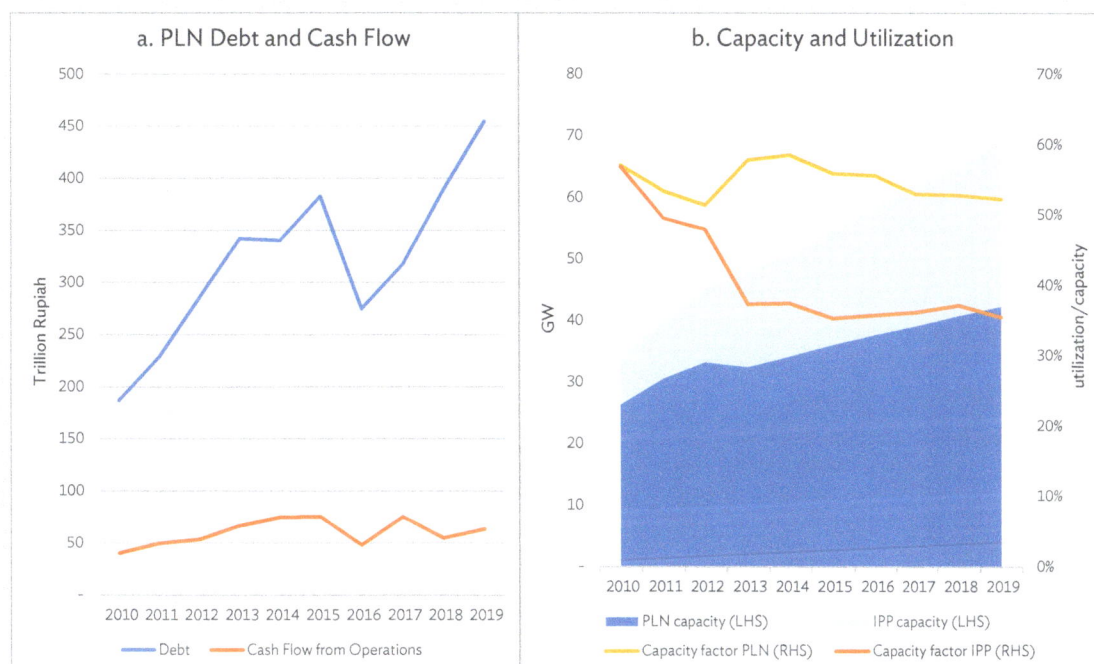

a. PLN Debt and Cash Flow

b. Capacity and Utilization

GW = gigawatt, IPP = independent power plant, LHS = left-hand scale, PLN = Perusahaan Listrik Negara (State Electricity Company), RHS = right-hand scale.

Source: Asian Development Bank calculations using data from the Ministry of State-Owned Enterprises.

In 2014 President Joko Widodo announced plans to increase Indonesia's power generation capacity to 85 gigawatts (GW) by 2019, from a baseline of 50.4 GW. Electricity generation capacity reached 69.6 GW in 2019, behind targets but representing close to a 40% expansion in capacity. To finance this additional capacity, PLN has taken on debt. An asset revaluation in 2015 saw PLN's equity soar (from Rp164 trillion in 2014 to Rp848 trillion in 2015), which PLN has since leveraged (see figure). PLN inked many power purchase agreements with independent producers for take-or-pay schemes under which PLN will be transferred ownership of independent power plants in the future. PLN's debt burden stood at Rp340 trillion in 2014, and by 2019 reached Rp454 trillion.[c] The additional capacity has, however, not been fully taken advantage of as demand growth has lagged behind expectations. The utilization rate or the share of total capacity used, has fallen for both PLN and independent power plants since 2014 (see figure). PLN's cash flow from operations has remained flat despite the increase in capacity and need to finance a growing debt burden.

This rapid increase in debt and slow growth in demand pose concerns for PLN's short-term viability and its ability to meet tomorrow's challenges. A debt-burdened PLN may face greater difficulties transitioning toward more sustainable energy sources while also meeting Indonesia's growing demand for power. PLN's production is dependent on fossil fuels, with coal dominating production at 50.7%, followed by gas at 26%, hydropower at 7%, and oil at 7.4%, with small amounts of production from other sources.[d] To control costs, PLN has begun to use a lower quality of coal, which has manifested in falling efficiency implying increased emissions per unit of energy (footnote b). Coal has been displacing cleaner alternatives, with PLN cancelling the majority of the 70 renewable energy power purchase agreements signed in 2017 (footnote a).

[a] Asian Development Bank. 2020. *Indonesia Energy Sector Assessment, Strategy, and Road Map—Update.* Manila.

[b] Institute for Essential Services Reform (IESR). 2019. *Indonesia's Coal Dynamics: Toward a Just Energy Transition.* Jakarta.

[c] By September 2020, PLN's debt had reached Rp490 trillion, per data from the Ministry of State-Owned Enterprises.

[d] PLN. 2020. *PLN Statistics 2019.* Jakarta.

Source: Asian Development Bank

36.   **Subsidies to state-owned enterprises.** Other PSOs often receive compensation in the form of production subsidies, which generally take the form of cost-plus margin mechanisms in which SOEs are reimbursed based on the cost of production plus an additional sum. This structure is typical but can potentially disincentivize efficiency. This is because SOEs both receive more money when they accrue greater costs and because private firms are disadvantaged as they cannot compete with the subsidized price offered by SOEs. Further, frequently late government payment of subsidies means that SOEs need to seek financing to bridge their working capital requirements. Late payments also have the impact of increasing the costs of PSOs for SOEs, as when SOEs take loans to compensate for late payments they are often not compensated for the cost of financing. Late payments of subsidies have also resulted in some SOEs missing payments to other SOEs.[57] Over 2015–2019, SOE subsidies averaged Rp158 trillion per year or roughly 7.7% of government expenditures (Figure 7). By far the largest subsidies, accounting for more than 95% of the total in 2019, are the fuel, electricity, and fertilizer subsidies. The structure of these subsidies and poor targeting create inefficiencies. Production subsidies for fertilizer, in particular, have been criticized for their cost and distortionary impacts on markets.[58] The fertilizer SOE, Pupuk, is reimbursed on a cost-plus basis, meaning that the cost of selling below market rates is made up by the government in addition to a 7% bonus.[59] The existence of a production subsidy limits Pupuk's incentives to produce efficiently, as it faces no private competition at its subsidized price point, and leaves little incentive to innovate. The subsidy is estimated to lead to extra agricultural production worth just half of the cost of the subsidy, while farmers overuse the cheap fertilizer (depressing yields in some cases).[60] President Joko Widodo has expressed criticism of the fertilizer subsidy structure.[61] Challenges with targeting also mean that these subsidies often do not go to the

Figure 7: Subsidies to State-Owned Enterprises as Share of Government Expenditure

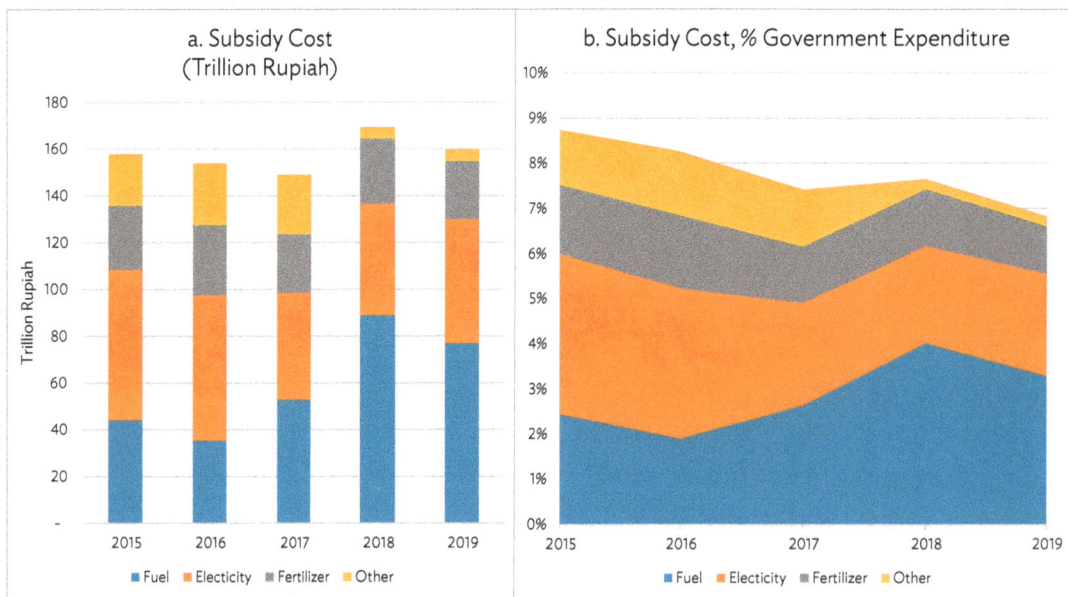

Rp = rupiah.

Source: Asian Development Bank calculation based on data from Ministry of State-Owned Enterprises and Statistics Indonesia (Badan Pusat Statistik).

[57]   ADB. 2015. *Fossil Fuels Subsidies in Indonesia: Trends, Impacts, Reforms.* Manila.
[58]   OECD. 2015. *Indonesia Policy Brief: Agriculture.* Paris.
[59]   AIPEG. The Fertilizer Sector and Subsidy Policy in Indonesia. Unpublished.
[60]   C. G. Osorio et al. 2011. Who is Benefiting from the Fertilizer Subsidies in Indonesia? *Policy Research Working Paper 5758.* Washington, DC.: World Bank.
[61]   A. B. Bardan. 2021. Ada Yang Tidak Beres, Jokowi Minta Subsidi Pupuk Dievaluasi (Something's Not Right – Jokowi Asks for the Fertilizer Subsidy to be Evaluated). *Kontan.* 11 January. Jakarta.

intended recipients, a problem that stakeholders have attributed to a lack of reliable data to guide disbursements to the intended recipients. The poor are estimated to only receive 20% of kerosene and liquefied petroleum gas subsidies, 3% of diesel subsidies, and 15% of the electricity subsidy.[62] Regarding fertilizers, 60% of the subsidies benefit the largest 40% of farmers and over 30% of subsidized fertilizer goes to nontargeted producers.

37.   **Implicit subsidies and guarantees.** SOEs may also receive "implicit" subsidies from the government, which represent foregone profits compared to expected performance (footnote 37). Allowing SOEs to not cover their risk-weighted cost of capital is equivalent to a subsidy, as an SOE that is not covering its risk-weighted cost of capital can be viewed as wasting government resources and worsening overall macroeconomic performance.[63] These implicit subsidies are often tied to the developmental role of SOEs, which are often instructed to take on unprofitable projects for which SOEs are not explicitly or fully compensated. If they are not compensated, the losses manifest in the destruction of capital, low revenues, or lower than efficient dividends. Building on prior analysis, this diagnostic provides a more precise estimate of implicit subsidies to Indonesia's SOEs based on emerging market ROE at a sector–year level (see Appendix 3 for more details).[64] Over the 2015–2018 period (following the

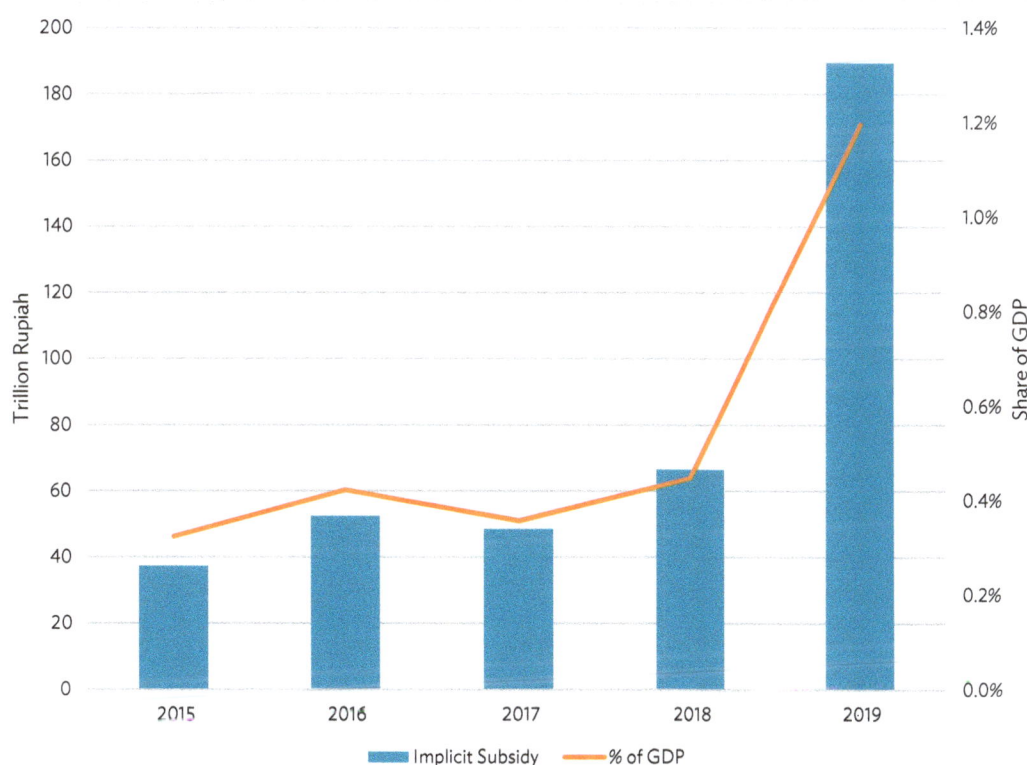

Figure 8: Implicit Subsidies to State-Owned Enterprises

GDP = gross domestic product.

Source: Asian Development Bank calculations using data from the Ministry of State-Owned Enterprises and Damodaran Online. Data: Current and Data: Archives. Accessed January 2021.

---

[62]   World Bank. 2020. *Indonesia Public Expenditure Review 2020: Spending for Better Results.* Jakarta.
[63]   AIPEG. Implicit Subsidies to Indonesia's SOEs are Creating Significant Risks to Indonesia's Economy. Unpublished.
[64]   Prior analysis by AIPEG assumed a uniform benchmark ROE of 12%. By relaxing this assumption and accounting for variation in ROE across sectors and years, this provides a more accurate estimate of implicit subsidies. Appendix 3 has more details.

2015 revaluation of SOE assets), implicit subsidies to SOEs have averaged roughly Rp50 trillion, about 0.4% of GDP (Figure 8). Implicit subsidies spiked to near Rp190 trillion in 2019, or nearly 1.2% of GDP. SOEs also benefit from implicit guarantees, wherein the market perceives a state commitment to settle SOE debts.[65] These implicit guarantees can become explicit, as in the case of Jiwasraya where the government stepped in to backstop the struggling insurer.

38.   **Overall budget impact of state-owned enterprises**. Expenditures on SOEs are large, but SOEs also contribute to the state budget. Dividends paid by SOEs have generally contributed roughly 2.5% of the government budget, exceeding the total value of equity injections in every year except for 2015 and 2016 (Figure 9). However, several SOEs pay dividends to the government even while receiving large equity injections (most notably PLN), a sign that these dividend payments likely exceed the capacity of these firms to pay. Taxes paid by SOEs averaged 12% of government revenues from 2010 to 2019 while explicit subsidies to SOEs averaged roughly 8% of expenditures from 2015–2020.[66] Accounting for the precise cost of SOEs is difficult, as SOEs would continue to pay taxes if privatized and subsidy expenditures can be best interpreted as government spending on policy goals rather than a specifically SOE-related expense.[67] The balance of equity injections and dividends alone may seem to imply that SOEs are a net positive for the state budget, but the situation is complicated by the various other costs created by state ownership, such as implicit subsidies, and the impacts of state ownership on the macroeconomy. As such, the overall impact of SOEs on the government budget is difficult to quantify precisely.

Figure 9: State-Owned Enterprise Dividends Paid and Equity Injections Received

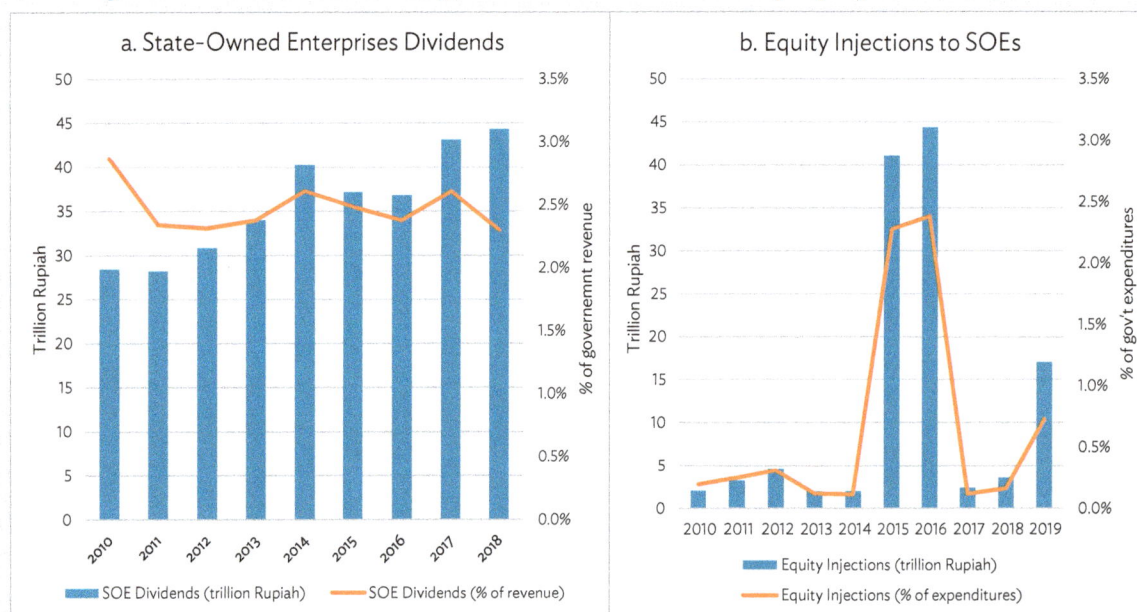

SOE = state-owned enterprise.

Source: Asian Development Bank calculations using data from the Ministry of State-Owned Enterprises and Statistics Indonesia (BPS).

---

[65] P. Cabrera, J. Oriol, and C. Moskovits. 2020. *Valuation of Credit Guarantees to State-Owned Enterprises.* Washington, DC.: Inter-American Development Bank.

[66] Data provided by the MSOE.

[67] Regarding taxes, while there are differences in the structure of taxes paid by SOEs, a private firm of similar performance would pay largely the same amount of taxes. As such, taxes paid by SOEs should not be considered a specific benefit to the state of firm ownership (unlike dividends). Likewise, the government could offer subsidies to achieve policy goals without relying on SOEs. Inefficiencies within SOEs may contribute to the high cost of some subsidies, but the specific cost associated with delivering subsidies through SOEs is difficult to estimate precisely.

IV. Current State-Owned Enterprises' Reform Proposals and Coronavirus Disease Pandemic Context

39. The MSOE has undertaken several reform actions with the aim of increasing the professionalism and independence of the MSOE and improving SOE performance in recent years. The MSOE has recently been reorganized and set ambitious reform goals under a new SOE minister with substantial private-sector expertise. These ambitious reform goals have been impacted by the COVID-19 pandemic, which has had an immediate and mixed impact on SOEs. SOEs are a key part of the government's fiscal and public health response. While the new MSOE minister was also appointed as the implementing chair of the Policy Committee on Handling COVID-19 and National Economic Recovery in July 2020, reform of SOEs remains a high priority.

Figure 10: Ministry of State-Owned Enterprises Priority Areas

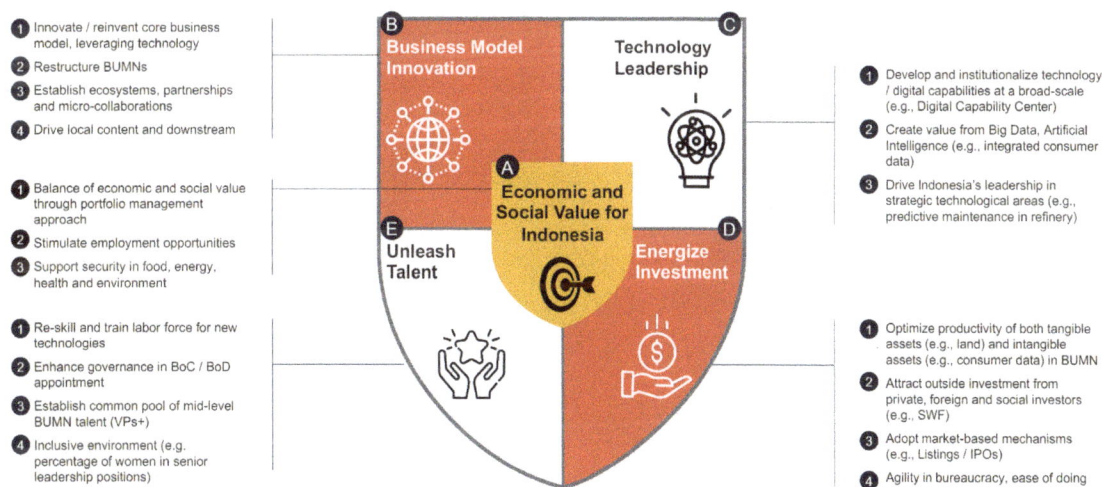

1 Innovate / reinvent core business model, leveraging technology
2 Restructure BUMNs
3 Establish ecosystems, partnerships and micro-collaborations
4 Drive local content and downstream

1 Balance of economic and social value through portfolio management approach
2 Stimulate employment opportunities
3 Support security in food, energy, health and environment

1 Re-skill and train labor force for new technologies
2 Enhance governance in BoC / BoD appointment
3 Establish common pool of mid-level BUMN talent (VPs+)
4 Inclusive environment (e.g. percentage of women in senior leadership positions)

B Business Model Innovation
C Technology Leadership
A Economic and Social Value for Indonesia
E Unleash Talent
D Energize Investment

1 Develop and institutionalize technology / digital capabilities at a broad-scale (e.g., Digital Capability Center)
2 Create value from Big Data, Artificial Intelligence (e.g., integrated consumer data)
3 Drive Indonesia's leadership in strategic technological areas (e.g., predictive maintenance in refinery)

1 Optimize productivity of both tangible assets (e.g., land) and intangible assets (e.g., consumer data) in BUMN
2 Attract outside investment from private, foreign and social investors (e.g., SWF)
3 Adopt market-based mechanisms (e.g., Listings / IPOs)
4 Agility in bureaucracy, ease of doing business

BOC = Board of Commissioners, BOD = Board of Directors, BUMN = State-Owned Enterprises.
Source: Government of Indonesia, Ministry of State-Owned Enterprises.

40. **Ministry of State-Owned Enterprises priority areas.** The MSOE has adopted five priority areas (Figure 10), many of which highlight the ministry's interest in reform: (A) increasing economic and social value for Indonesia, especially in the fields of food security, energy, and health; (B) restructuring business models through ecosystem development, cooperation, consideration of stakeholders needs, and focus on core business; (C) leading globally in strategic technology and institutionalizing digital capabilities such as data management, advanced analytics, big data, artificial intelligence, and others; (D) optimizing asset values and building a healthy investment ecosystem; and (E) educating and training the workforce, developing quality human capital, professionalizing governance and human resources selection systems. Furthermore, cooperation between SOEs and the private sector is being actively encouraged (Box 6).

Box 6: Cooperation Between State-Owned Enterprises and the Private Sector

State-owned enterprises (SOEs) have successfully pursued several strategic partnerships with the private sector in recent years. This trend represents a change of direction from a prior strategy of "SOE Synergy," which emphasized close cooperation among SOEs.[a] Cooperation with the private sector is important for building SOE capacity and has positive impacts on SOE performance.[b] Following is a non-exhaustive list of recent partnerships in Indonesia:

- SOEs including state oil and gas company Pertamina, electricity distribution monopoly PLN, mining holding company PT Mining Industry Indonesia (MIND ID), and mining firm PT Antam have established Indonesia Battery Corporation (IBC), an electric vehicle (EV) battery holding company.[c] IBC has received investment interest from several multinational firms in the sector, and has announced investment deals with major EV battery producers including the People's Republic of China's CATL (worth $5.2 billion) and the Republic of Korea's LG Chem ($9.8 billion).[d] As Indonesia is home to nearly a fifth of the world's reserves of nickel, a key component for EV batteries, the potential to spur technology transfers through international cooperation can support the development of this growing industry in Indonesia.

- PLN has signed a power purchase agreement with Masdar, one of the world's leading renewable energy companies, to build the first floating solar photovoltaic plant in Indonesia.[e] The plant will have a capacity of 145 megawatts. The project investment has an estimated value of $129 million.

- SOEs have cooperated with the private sector in developing the Jakarta Mass Rapid Transit (MRT), the first underground train system in Jakarta and a much-needed transit option for Indonesia's densely populated and often congested capital city. Infrastructure-focused SOEs such as Wijaya Karya and Adhi Karya have cooperated with Japanese firms while working on the Jakarta MRT and its extensions.[f] Wijaya Karya has expanded its partnerships with Japanese firms through the formation of a joint engineering and research institute.[g] The experience gained through these partnerships helped to support construction on the Jakarta MRT, and has enabled infrastructure SOEs to increase their capabilities and experience in working on transit infrastructure. Wijaya Karya is currently the only international contractor working on extensions of the Taipei,China MRT alongside local firms, demonstrating the benefits of capability development spurred by international cooperation on the Jakarta MRT.

- Telkom launched a joint venture with Singtel in 2015, with the aim of providing applications for commercial companies and co-branded SIM cards.[i] This cooperation builds on a close relationship between Singtel and Telkom Indonesia. Telkomsel, the subsidiary of Telkom, which is the largest wireless carrier in Indonesia, is itself a joint venture between Telkom Indonesia (holding a 65% majority share) and Singtel (holding a 35% minority share). Singtel is majority-owned by Temasek, Singapore's successful SOE holding company.

[a] Government of Indonesia. *KBUMN Annual Report 2015*. Jakarta.

[b] World Bank. 2014. *Corporate Governance of State-Owned Enterprises: A Toolkit*. Washington, DC.

[c] *The Jakarta Post*. 2021. Indonesia Launches EV Battery Holding Company. 29 March.

[d] S. Tani. 2021. Indonesian State Companies Set Up EV Battery Developer. *NikkeiAsia*. 27 March.

[e] I. Shumkov. 2020. Masdar, PLN Unit Set Up JV to Tackle Floating Solar Development in Indonesia. *Renewables Now*. 17 December.

[f] *Tempo*. 2012. Wika Gandeng Jepang Bangun MRT di Jakarta (Wika Collaborates with Japan to Build MRT in Jakarta). 10 May; S. Bahfein. 2021. Adhi Karya Berambisi Rajai Sektor Konstruksi Kereta Api di Indonesia (Adhi Karya Aims to Dominate the Railway Construction Sector in Indonesia). *Kompas*. 1 May.

[g] E. Simorangkir. 2017. Kembangkan Teknologi Konstruksi, Wika Belajar dari Jepan (Developing Construction Technology, Wika Learns from Japan). *DetikFinance*. 22 July.

[i] Y. Hardiyan. 2015. Telkom Bakal Gandeng Singtel Bentuk Usaha Patungan (Telkom to Cooperate with Singtel to Form a Joint Venture). *Bisnis*. 22 June.

Source: Asian Development Bank.

41.   **Ongoing reform actions.** Specific ongoing reform efforts include the following:

- **Changes to the Ministry of State-Owned Enterprises.** The MSOE was reorganized in 2019 with the creation of 12 sector clusters organized into 2 portfolios of 6 clusters, each overseen by a vice-minister (Appendix 4). These clusters are: (i) energy (including oil and gas), (ii) minerals and coal, (iii) fertilizer and food, (iv) plantations and forestry, (v) manufacturing (including defense), (vi) health, (vii) finance, (viii) logistics, (ix) infrastructure, (x) tourism and related industries, (xi) insurance and pensions, and (xii) telecommunications and media. Stakeholders at SOEs felt that this new structure has allowed for more effective oversight. In addition to the new structure, the new minister also brought in new staff with substantial private-sector expertise, including the new vice-ministers. Several stakeholders at SOEs appreciated the presence of more private-sector professionals at the MSOE, which they believed enabled a more conducive environment for SOE success.

- **Changes to state-owned enterprises.** Reforms have sought to allow SOEs more freedom to enter into operation agreements with the private sector through the implementation of a limited concession scheme (under which SOE assets can be leased for operation by private firms). SOE restructuring and corporate governance reforms have continued. The MSOE has also sought to adopt longer-term plans for its holdings by creating cluster-level master plans aligned with the RPJMN 2020–2024 based on a 5-year time horizon, which are then translated to 1-year plans for each SOE. This planning process is done in collaboration with SOEs, with special provisions for SOEs that are publicly traded. The MSOE is seeking to increase the human capital within SOEs, improve human resource practices within the SOE sector, and increase standardization. This agenda has involved the adoption of unified core values (AKHLAK, an acronym for "morals"), a focus on the acquisition of new talent and talent management, unification of SOE education programs, a more standardized system of performance assessments, and a mandate that all SOEs receive audits from a list of qualified audit firms. Some reforms to hiring within SOEs have been implemented, including caps on the number of aides and a limit on the maximum monthly salaries for expert staff advisors.[68] The MSOE has also set targets to increase the share of women on SOE boards to 15% by 2024, from 11% in 2021.[69]

42.   **Active proposals for future reform.** The MSOE is continuing to pursue consolidations of SOEs to reduce the number of its holdings. It is also exploring greater disclosure for SOEs implementing public service obligations, including the national strategic projects. There are ongoing discussions on permitting the MSOE to retain a portion of SOE dividends to fund part of its operations and to strengthen its incentives to improve SOE performance. Stakeholders within the MSOE have also discussed two separate entities in development to alleviate capacity constraints within the ministry. One of these entities is a strategic delivery unit, which will be staffed by SOEs and the MSOE but will draw its budget from SOEs and is intended to support the implementation and monitoring of priority reforms. The other is a global self-service entity that will provide funding, drawn from SOE budgets, to hire outside consultants. Recent changes in the composition of the Privatization Committee have also opened the door to potential public offerings or sales of state companies.[70] The MSOE minister has also discussed potential future sales of smaller SOEs.[71]

---

[68]   *The Jakarta Post*. 2020. Ministry to Limit SOEs' Expert Staff Numbers, Salaries. 8 September.

[69]   L. Afifa. 2021. Minister Erick Thohir Aims to Boost Women's Leadership in SOEs. *Tempo*. 7 April.

[70]   Government of Indonesia. 2021. Keputusan Presiden (KEPPRES) 2/2021 (Amendment to Presidential Decree Number 47 of 2014 concerning the Public Company [Persero] Privatization Committee). Jakarta.

[71]   *Kompas*. 2021. Erick Thohir akan Lakukan Swastanisasi BUMN yang Pendapatannya di Bawah Rp 50 Miliar (Erick Thohir Will Privatize SOEs with Incomes Below Rp 50 Billion). 5 March.

43.   **Coronavirus disease crisis impacts on state-owned enterprises.** The impact of the COVID-19 pandemic on SOEs has varied widely by sector, with the performance and viability of some critical SOEs suffering while other SOEs weathered the crisis better than expected (Box 7). SOEs involved in infrastructure construction have been hit hard by the pandemic given their highly leveraged balance sheets and project delays. From the start of the pandemic in March 2020 to January 2021, compared with the preceding 9-month period, profits were down Rp3.8 trillion for Waskita Karya (which registered a loss of Rp2.6 trillion in the 9 months from March 2020), Rp1.3 trillion for Wijaya Karya, Rp518 million for PTPP, and Rp336 million for Adhi Karya.[72] Garuda Indonesia was also hit hard by the pandemic, registering losses of Rp16.0 trillion over the 9 months from March 2020. However, other SOEs are set to recover rapidly from the crisis, particularly financial SOEs and mining and minerals SOEs which have seen their stock prices climb rapidly. Most SOE clusters kept their gearing ratios at levels similar to those before the pandemic and some even managed to still make a profit in 2020 (Box 7). Understandably, only tourism SOEs seem to have suffered a substantial reduction in income and equity levels. SOEs have also been called upon to play a key role in the economic recovery and public health response. This has taken the form of both explicitly funded PSOs, such as large programs routed through state banks (see discussion below), as well as other forms of support such as Telkom's role in developing technological solutions for vaccine distribution in partnership with Biofarma, the state pharmaceutical holding company, which has been producing Sinovac doses for local distribution.[73]

44.   **State-owned enterprises as conduit and recipient of coronavirus disease response funds.** SOEs have been made a key pillar of Indonesia's economic stimulus and recovery efforts, with the use of SOEs as conduits of government support to the economy well illustrating their potential use as agents of development. Under the National Economic Recovery (*Pemulihan Ekonomi Nasional,* or PEN) plan, Rp128.2 trillion was authorized for a variety of economic support measures linked to SOEs. The bulk of this funding (Rp116.6 trillion) was directed to the four major SOE banks (Bank Rakyat Indonesia [BRI], Bank Negara Indonesia [BNI], Bank Mandiri, and Bank Tabungan Negara [BTN]) and two other nonbank financial SOEs (Permodalan Nasional Madani [PNM] and Pegadaian) to fund government initiatives such as a salary subsidy program (Rp28.2 trillion), subsidies to allow reduced interest payments (Rp11.3 trillion), support to small and micro-sized businesses (Rp22.5 trillion), and credit guarantees (Rp0.9 trillion).[74] The PEN plan also authorized Rp11.5 trillion to PLN for increased household electricity subsidies. Beyond the PEN expenditures, a total of Rp50.7 trillion of additional support to SOEs, composed of back payments for subsidies, equity injections, and loans, was authorized for 2020 under several presidential regulations. These support include money for Biofarma (Rp2.0 trillion) to aid with vaccine production and distribution, loans to state airline Garuda Indonesia (Rp8.5 trillion), and equity injections for the highly leveraged construction firm Hutama Karya (Rp11.0 trillion).[75] The standard annual subsidies to SOEs amounted to Rp139 trillion in 2020, a decline from the 2019 amount of Rp159 trillion, mostly due to a decrease in the gas subsidy (from Rp76.8 trillion to Rp55.4 trillion) tied to depressed fuel prices in 2020. The impacts of these emergency response programs on SOE financial health, given the financial stresses facing some SOEs entering the crisis, should be monitored carefully to minimize any potential negative impacts on Indonesia's recovery.

---

[72]   MSOE data.

[73]   *Jakarta Globe.* 2021. Indonesia Administers Sinovac Vaccine Manufactured by Bio Farma. 19 February.

[74]   MSOE data. Numbers reflect approvals, not disbursements.

[75]   H. Hanggi. 2020. Bio Farma to Receive Rp2 Trillion in State Capital Injections. *Tempo.* 6 November; M. Parama and R. Rahman. 2020. House Approves Rp 8.5t in Convertible Bond for Ailing Garuda. *The Jakarta Post.* 16 July; Government of Indonesia, Cabinet. 2020. 12 SOEs to Receive Stimulus as Part of Economic Recovery Programs. Jakarta.

Box 7: State-Owned Enterprises Cluster Performance during the Coronavirus Disease Pandemic

The coronavirus disease (COVID-19) pandemic struck Indonesia's economy sharply in 2020 with likely scarring effects well into the future. It was an unexpected shock that hit all sectors of the economy—albeit not equally harshly—with some sectors contracting by more than 50% like air travel. Although the shock of the pandemic impedes assessment of the recent performance of state-owned enterprises (SOEs), it does offer a useful glimpse to their resilience to risks.

The following figure shows shows the debt–to–equity ratios of each SOE cluster in 2019 and in the third quarter of 2021. The clusters on the left column of the graph kept their debt–to–equity balance roughly stable. PT Danareksa-PPA as well as the insurance cluster—which had relatively high debt–to–equity ratios before the pandemic—even saw a substantial reduction in their headline gearing ratio. The tourism cluster, understandably, suffered from a negative equity balance as of the third quarter of 2021.

Debt–to–Equity Ratio by SOE Cluster, 2019 and 2021

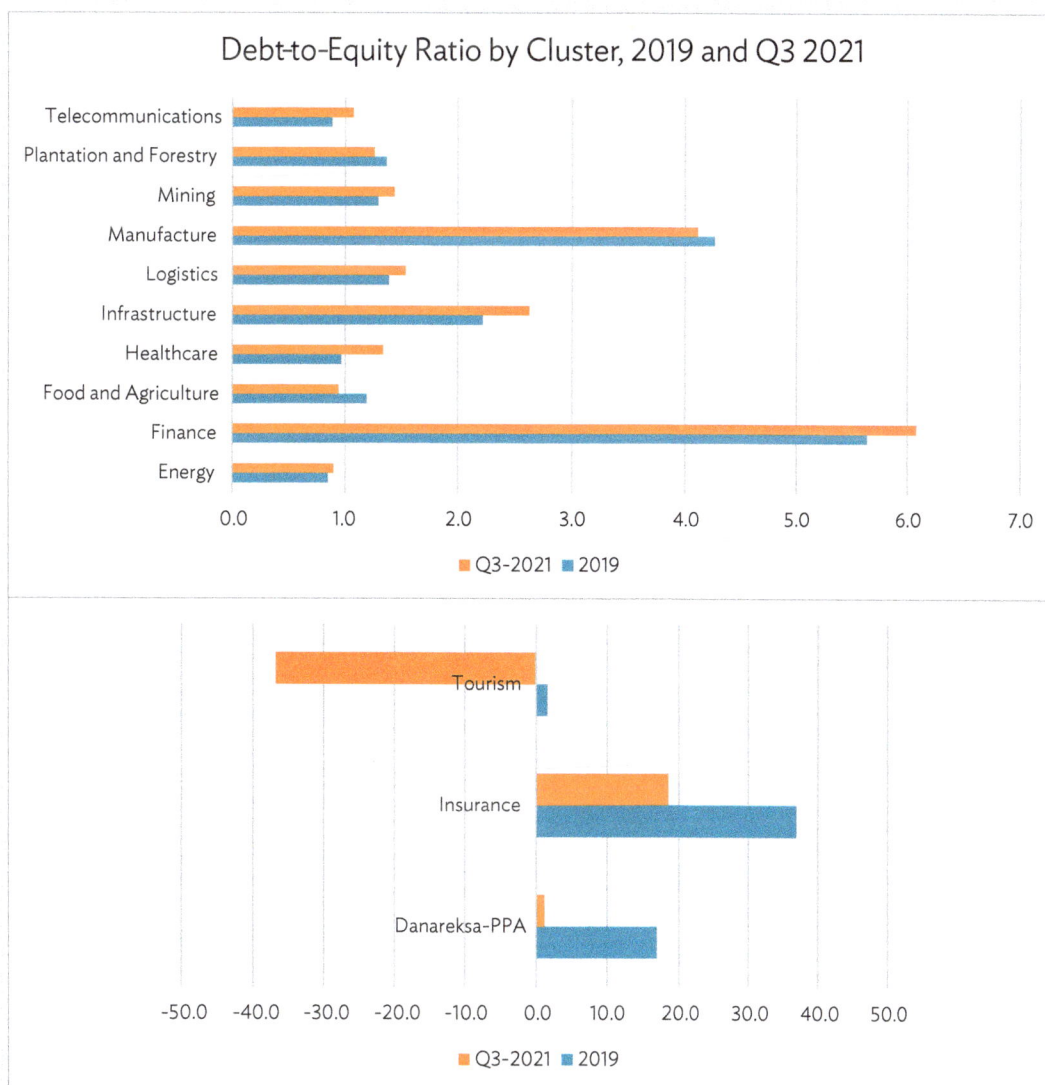

PPA = Perusahaan Pengelola Aset (Persero), SOE = state-owned enterprise.

Source: Asian Development Bank calculations using data from the Ministry of State-Owned Enterprises.

continued on next page

Box 7 *continued*

The next figure shows the net income of SOE clusters from 2018 to the third quarter of 2021. The financial services, healthcare, infrastructure, logistics, and tourism clusters saw a reduction in net income in 2020. The way in which the pandemic affected clusters differently points to the distinct risks each cluster faces. It suggests that overseeing the management of risk would be optimized by tailoring a different approach for every cluster, as each cluster not only has different risks inherent to their business but also differs in how they are able to manage uncertainty and downturn. In this regard, the Ministry of State-Owned Enterprises is developing a comprehensive risk management guideline for SOEs in its portfolio. The guideline considers each SOE's unique circumstances, which is a step in the right direction toward more effectively managing SOE risks.

Net Income by SOE Cluster, 2018 to 2021

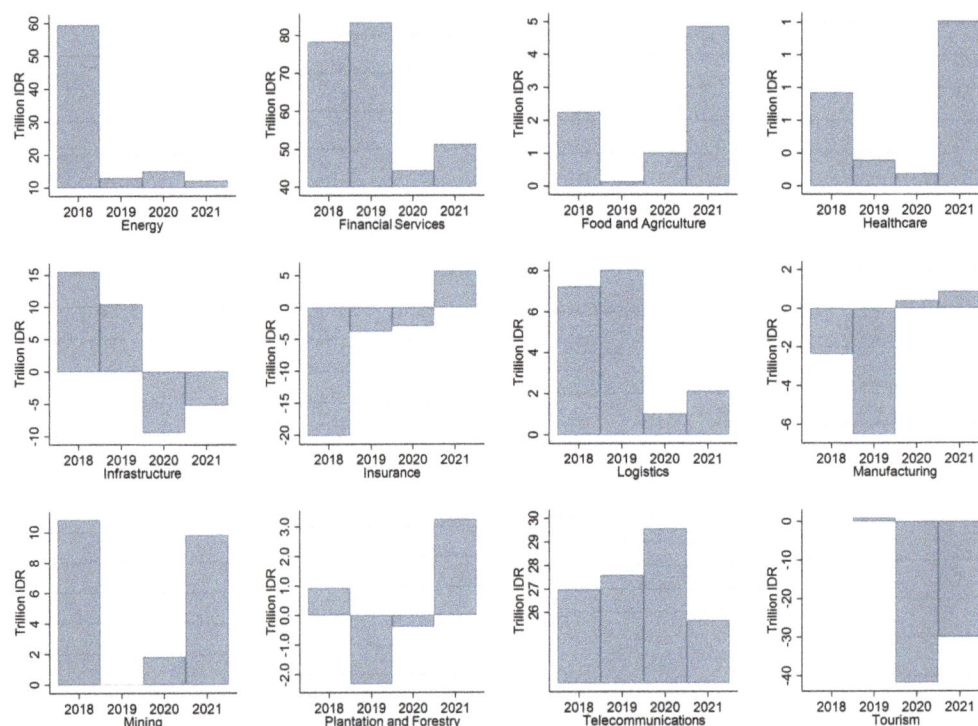

SOE = state-owned enterprise.

Source: Asian Development Bank calculations using data from the Ministry of State-Owned Enterprises.

45.   **Indonesia Investment Authority's potential impact on state-owned enterprises.** A newly created investment entity intended to maximize investments to support sustainable development, the Indonesia Investment Authority (INA), may have immediate and long-run impacts on SOEs. Created as part of the Job Creation Law (commonly referred to as the Omnibus Bill) enacted in 2020, the INA is mandated to (i) optimize assets (including shares in SOEs and by operating SOE assets), (ii) attract investments by spurring co-investment with overseas and local partners, and (iii) play an active role in improving Indonesia's investment climate. Though INA is not an SOE, the MSOE minister will serve on the INA's supervisory board alongside the MoF minister and three independent board members. The fund has been capitalized with a combination of cash and SOE shares, and is seeking additional investments from international and local sources. The mandate of the INA, as well as the presence of the SOE minister on the board, signal that it could become a key tool for improving the return on SOE assets, though there are still questions about the potential impact and aims of this new entity.

V. Constraints to State-Owned Enterprise Performance and Additional Proposed Reforms

46. The mixed performance of Indonesian SOEs is the result of several constraints, many relating to areas where Indonesia's SOE governance framework diverges from international good practices. For example, there is a need for the MSOE to focus further on setting good governance standards and empowering qualified and responsible boards while increasing its own capacity and capabilities. In addition, the weaknesses in the structure of PSO compensation and a limited independence and weak market incentives for many viable SOEs create challenges for SOEs. In several instances, Indonesia's SOE governance framework falls short of best practices as defined in the OECD framework (Appendix 6) and discussed in the preceding sections. These areas of divergence form the basis for many of the key constraints identified in this diagnostic, and the proposed recommendations aim at addressing these areas of divergence.

47. The MSOE's ongoing reform actions address several of the issues facing SOEs, but there is scope to further improve SOE governance and performance in Indonesia. Aligned with this diagnostic's three-pillar framework, the following section discusses key constraints in each of the three pillars and, informed by international frameworks and consultations with key stakeholders, suggests several avenues for further reform (Figure 11) building on the ongoing initiatives outlined in Section IV. By strengthening the MSOE, reforming SOE–government relations,

Figure 11: Additional Proposed Reforms

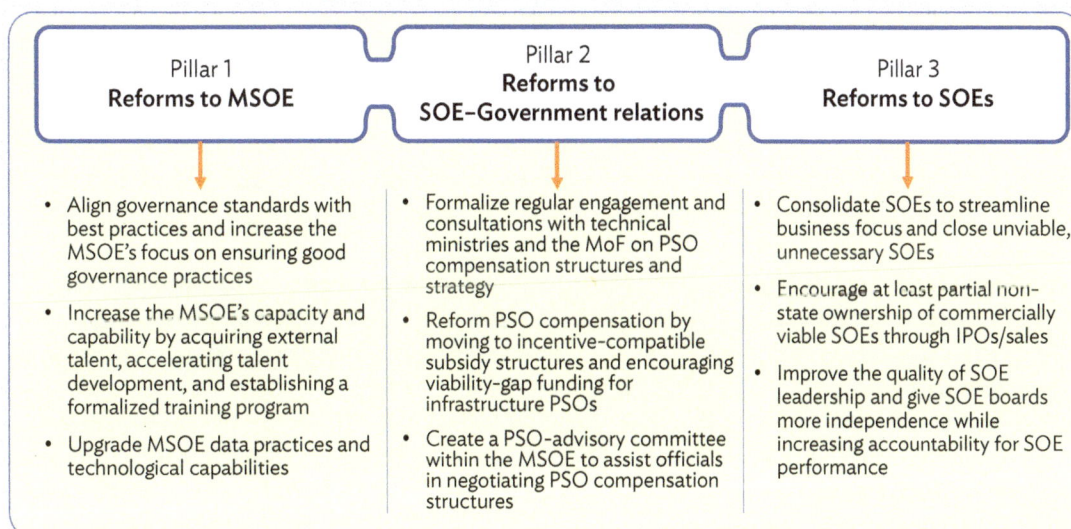

Pillar 1 **Reforms to MSOE**	Pillar 2 **Reforms to SOE–Government relations**	Pillar 3 **Reforms to SOEs**
• Align governance standards with best practices and increase the MSOE's focus on ensuring good governance practices	• Formalize regular engagement and consultations with technical ministries and the MoF on PSO compensation structures and strategy	• Consolidate SOEs to streamline business focus and close unviable, unnecessary SOEs
• Increase the MSOE's capacity and capability by acquiring external talent, accelerating talent development, and establishing a formalized training program	• Reform PSO compensation by moving to incentive-compatible subsidy structures and encouraging viability-gap funding for infrastructure PSOs	• Encourage at least partial non-state ownership of commercially viable SOEs through IPOs/sales
• Upgrade MSOE data practices and technological capabilities	• Create a PSO-advisory committee within the MSOE to assist officials in negotiating PSO compensation structures	• Improve the quality of SOE leadership and give SOE boards more independence while increasing accountability for SOE performance

IPO = initial public offering, MoF = Ministry of Finance, MSOE = Ministry of State-Owned Enterprises, SOE = state-owned enterprise, PSO = public service obligation.

Source: Asian Development Bank.

and increasing the independence and viability of SOEs, Indonesia's SOEs can better contribute to the recovery from the COVID-19 pandemic and support Indonesia's continued development. To deepen and institutionalize the SOEs' reform, Indonesia should also consider updating the 2003 SOE Law to bring it more in line with international best practices.

A. Pillar 1: Ministry of State-Owned Enterprises

48.   **Identified Constraint I: Deviations from good governance practices negatively impact state-owned enterprise performance.** The MSOE should avoid taking actions that could negatively impact SOEs, such as rapidly changing SOE leadership, selecting individuals for roles for which they may lack sufficient qualifications, and preventing SOEs from acting independently (para. 33). Several interventions by MSOE are intended to help SOEs meet higher standards. However, they sometimes lead to counterproductive results due to excessive interventions. Approvals from the MSOE are often slow, requiring numerous reviews across the ministry, with the focus on short-term goals. This focus on short-term objectives rather than long-term planning is a risk in SOE management, and has resulted in boards with little autonomy that are not empowered to operate SOEs independent of the state.[76] In addition, requiring a large number of approvals limits SOE boards' ability to operate independently and slows down SOE dynamism.

49.   **Proposed Reform I: Align governance standards with best practices and increase the Ministry of State-Owned Enterprises' focus on ensuring good governance practices.** The MSOE could improve its oversight function and provide effective support for better SOE performance by focusing more on setting high governance standards and empowering qualified SOE boards. The MSOE should focus on achieving full implementation of the SOE Law throughout the SOE ecosystem, including to SOE subsidiaries (footnote 37). The MSOE should focus on applying good governance practices and ensuring the selection of well-qualified, independent boards for SOEs, and also empower boards of directors to run SOEs with minimal intervention while holding boards accountable for their performance.[77] Achieving public policy goals through SOEs should be done by clearly communicating policy needs to SOEs and allowing SOE boards to develop plans to meet these goals, rather than intervening in SOE operations and planning. Best practices suggest an iterative process wherein SOE management develops strategic plans in response to broad goals set and communicated by the state, rather than top-down planning. Such a planning process can be aligned with the MSOE's efforts to reform planning (as discussed in para. 41). With the building of MSOE's oversight capacity, it should also seek to reduce the number of approvals required of SOEs to allow for more autonomy. In line with an increase in SOE autonomy, disclosure and transparency requirements should be strengthened. In particular, regulations ensuring independent commissioners must be applied to SOE subsidiaries to enable them to fulfill their oversight function effectively.

50.   **Identified Constraint II: The Ministry of State-Owned Enterprises needs to strengthen its capacity and capability to carry out its mission.** The MSOE faces both capacity and capability constraints, with several stakeholders highlighting a mismatch between ministry aims and staff competencies in addition to the small size of the MSOE staffing. Less than 25% of MSOE staff possess a master's degree equivalent or higher, while slightly more than 25% of MSOE staff have less than a bachelor's degree equivalent.[78] The MSOE has historically not invested enough in developing or acquiring talent, and it tends to be staffed by civil servants without the private sector experience needed to manage commercial entities operating in the corporate sector. The MSOE requires staff that can contribute to fulfilling its mission as an ownership entity, including such aims as depoliticizing SOE

---

[76]   World Bank. 2006. *Held by the Visible Hand: The Challenge of SOE Corporate Governance for Emerging Markets.* Washington, DC.

[77]   OECD. 2015. *OECD Guidelines on Corporate Governance of State-Owned Enterprises.* Paris.

[78]   Internal data from the Ministry of State-Owned Enterprises.

decision-making, monitoring the appropriate performance indicators, ensuring that SOEs adhere to international best practices, and achieving other priorities aligned with its role as a responsible ownership entity.

51.   **Proposed Reform II: Increase the capacity and capability of the Ministry of State-Owned Enterprises by acquiring talent, accelerating talent development, and establishing formalized training programs.** The MSOE should be encouraged to increase its capacity to fulfill its oversight function by improving the skillset of its human resources and increasing the alignment with its mission of providing oversight for a variety of commercial enterprises operating across several sectors. The MSOE needs to hire officials with private sector experience, which will also mean that remunerations will need to be benchmarked to the private sector. The MSOE also has to exert greater effort to advance talent development within the ministry. It should set higher educational attainment qualifications for its staff, support current staff in pursuing advanced degrees, and set higher standards for officials at the director and assistant deputy level based on education and accomplishments. The MSOE should support executive education programs and secondments for its staff to help build competencies within the MSOE, and set up a formal program for training and talent development linked to career progression within the ministry. Improving the capabilities of the MSOE is the necessary basis for the effective implementation of a more centralized state ownership function.

52.   **Identified Constraint III: The Ministry of State-Owned Enterprises lacks complete data on many aspects of the state-owned enterprises ecosystem, particularly state-owned enterprise subsidiaries.** Timely and accurate data is key to ensuring the proper application of oversight and monitoring functions of the MSOE. The MSOE has invested in improving its data on SOEs, but data are imperfect and coverage was incomplete. In particular, the MSOE lacks visibility into SOE subsidiaries. The exact number and nature of SOE subsidiaries was unclear, as is their staffing and boards. This lack of data hinders efforts to properly apply governance standards throughout the SOE ecosystem. Data concerns also make it more difficult to deploy SOEs for achieving government policy objectives on subsidy targeting.

53.   **Proposed Reform III: Upgrade the data practices and technological capabilities of the Ministry of State-Owned Enterprises.** In line with the effort to improve the capability and capacity of the MSOE, data practices and standards set by the ministry should be upgraded so that more reliable data and analytics on SOE performance are available. This will enable better oversight and internal governance of SOEs.[79] The MSOE should seek to increase its capabilities to gather data and information on SOE subsidiaries to ensure relevant regulations are being applied, as advised in Proposed Reform I under this pillar. Increased staff capabilities can help these efforts. The MSOE should also be provided with the necessary budgetary resources to pursue these improvements.

B. Pillar 2: Government–State-Owned Enterprises Relations

54.   **Identified Constraint I: Misalignments, lack of coordination with line and technical ministries lead to inefficiencies.** Many SOEs are subject to oversight from numerous ministries beyond the MSOE and stakeholders have emphasized that coordination between ministries regarding SOEs and PSOs has been lacking (Appendix 1 has a list of the many ministries impacting SOEs by sector). The priorities of line and technical ministries with oversight of many PSOs and regulations are often in conflict with SOE financial health and

[79]   Asian Development Bank Institute. 2017. *Efficient Management of State-Owned Enterprises: Challenges and Opportunities.* Tokyo; World Bank. 2014. *Corporate Governance of State-Owned Enterprises: A Toolkit.* Washington, DC.

performance. Line and technical ministries set prices, rates, and regulations that directly impact SOEs offering PSOs without ensuring suitable PSO compensation structures or consulting with the MSOE. Subsidy payments from the MoF are frequently late, requiring debt financing of PSOs. These decisions, taken by ministries other than the MSOE, can create significant financial burdens for SOEs. This fragmented ecosystem undermines centralized SOE oversight, as recommended by the OECD.

55.   **Proposed Reform I: Formalize regular engagement and consultations with technical ministries and the Ministry of Finance on public service obligation compensation structures and strategy.** The MSOE is not the sole player involved in setting the PSO structure. Engagement across ministries on these issues must be strengthened, and the MSOE must have a greater role in the setting of policies that directly impact its holdings. The MSOE will need to develop an appropriate mechanism to monitor the SOE balance sheet on its public service obligations. Increased coordination between the MSOE and sector ministries can improve the alignment of incentives and ensure that long-term planning is aligned across ministries regarding SOEs. Improving the coordination across government ministries with impacts on SOEs can help improve performance by ensuring the MSOE and other ministries are aligned, increasing focus and consistency in SOE oversight (footnote 12).

56.   **Identified Constraint II: Public service obligation compensation structure limits private sector participation in government projects and the economy.** In addition to the downsides of using equity injections and production subsidies in terms of cost and efficiency, these PSO structures also ensure unequal competition between SOEs and the private sector (para. 34). Preference for equity injections makes it difficult for private sector firms to gain many infrastructure contracts, as equity injections are only feasible for state firms. Further, production subsidies mean consumers have a financial incentive to take advantage of subsidized products from SOEs at the expense of the private sector.

57.   **Proposed Reform II: Reform public service obligation compensation by moving to incentive-compatible subsidy structures and encouraging viability gap funding for infrastructure public service obligations.** Subsidies should be restructured to ensure better performance by both SOEs and increased private sector participation in the provision of these key goods.[80] Providing a subsidy directly to consumers, rather than a production subsidy, could greatly reduce the cost of the subsidy to the government, increase the incentive for SOEs to innovate and improve their production processes, while also better ensuring low prices for the intended targeted consumers. Viability gap funding for infrastructure PSOs, where the funding shortfall for constructing an infrastructure PSO is paid by the central government, is more sustainable for SOEs than equity injections and does not burden SOEs with bad debt.[81] Viability gap funding should be adopted for all such projects rather than equity injections. Accurately priced viability gap funding would also allow private firms to compete for these projects. All PSO structures must be agreed in advance and clearly communicated to SOE boards, who should be responsible to plan for implementation of the policy aim, to limit the impact on SOEs and reduce uncertainty. Ensuring that PSOs are properly compensated would enable the government to fully understand the true cost of these activities and weigh them against other policy priorities.[82]

58.   **Identified Constraint III: Public service obligations need to be structured better to reduce their long-term cost and impact on state-owned enterprises.** While PSOs can play a positive role in promoting developmental progress, the current structure of PSO compensation creates substantial risks and inefficiencies. Compensation for infrastructure PSOs has tended to be structured as equity injections, limiting on-budget

[80]   OECD. 2012. *Competitive Neutrality: Maintaining a Level Playing Field Between Public and Private Business.* Paris.
[81]   World Bank. Infrastructure Sector Assessment. Unpublished.
[82]   M. E. Rayess et al. 2019. Indonesia's Public Wealth: A Balance Sheet Approach to Fiscal Policy Analysis. *IMF Working Paper.* No. 19/81. Washington, DC.

expenditures for the government but negatively impacting SOE financial health (para. 35). Although production subsidies have been used to provide goods to the public at low cost, the structure of these subsidies incentivizes a high cost of production within SOEs, increasing costs to the government and rewarding poor productivity. Poorly planned PSOs may have ripple effects within the entire SOE ecosystem. For example, SOEs constructing infrastructure often borrow from state-owned banks. When the government places additional PSO requirements on already overstretched firms, this can impact their ability to repay state-owned banks on loans taken for other projects. As such, PSOs at one firm can negatively impact the ability of that firm to borrow for commercial purposes, or can destabilize state-owned banks if loans sour.

59.   **Proposed Reform III: Create a public service obligation advisory committee within the Ministry of State-Owned Enterprises to assist officials in negotiating public service obligation compensation structures.** At present, discussions over PSOs are handled on an ad hoc basis and there is no central coordinating body to support PSO negotiations within the MSOE. Given the importance of ensuring appropriate PSO compensation structures, the MSOE should create an advisory body to support these negotiations to improve its capacity in managing PSOs (footnote 12). Such a committee should be composed of experts with experience in PSO negotiations and awareness of the impact of PSOs on both SOEs and the broader economy, and should aim to help improve PSO compensation structures. The PSO advisory committee should help MSOE officials with cross-ministry engagement (para. 54). The government should be able to provide a more precise accounting of these costs, as recommended under best practices, and ensure that compensation is appropriately set and delivered reliably.

C. Pillar 3: State-Owned Enterprises

60.   **Identified Constraint I: Many state-owned enterprises may not be commercially viable.** While a relatively small share of SOE assets is linked to poorly performing firms (excluding PLN), these poorly performing "zombie" SOEs are difficult to close down due to a variety of institutional and political economy constraints (para. 25). In lieu of closing them down, some SOEs have been consolidated under larger SOEs. While structuring firms as holding companies, such as in the case of Pupuk and Perum Perhutani, does reduce the number of SOEs, additional measures will be needed to create viable business structures and improve SOE performance.

61.   **Proposed Reform I: Consolidate state-owned enterprises to streamline business focus and close unviable, unnecessary ones.** While continued clustering and consolidation can help reduce the overall number of SOEs and allow better performing SOEs to take over the assets of poorly performing ones, consolidation should aim to create viable firms. Aligned with the cluster approach, the creation of holding companies through consolidations may have benefits for SOEs as long as these holding companies have clear mandates and are transparent.[83] There are many cases where SOEs are not viable and should be closed down.[84] These SOEs tend to be small, provide little economic or social value, and their assets should be liquidated and transferred to more competitive firms or the government budgets. Recent changes in the Privatization Committee should aid efforts to pursue necessary divestments of unproductive firms. The smallest 75 SOEs accounted for just 2.3% of total SOE assets in 2019 (Table 1) while being overrepresented in the group of poor performers (Figure 12), making them comparatively easier targets for divestment than larger, more valuable firms. The MSOE should support divestments from small, largely unproductive firms that lack a clear rationale for state ownership (further discussions are in para. 63 and Appendix 3).

---

[83]   OECD. 2021. *OECD Economic Surveys: Indonesia.* Paris.

[84]   World Bank. 2014. *Corporate Governance of State-Owned Enterprises: A Toolkit.* Washington, DC.; IMF. 2016. *Fiscal Policy: How to Improve the Financial Oversight of Public Corporations.* Washington, DC. November.

Figure 12: Quadrant Evaluation of State-Owned Enterprises

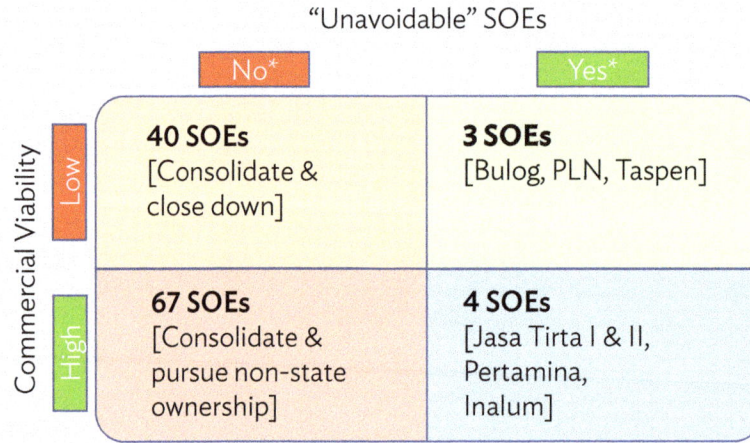

"Unavoidable" SOEs

	No*	Yes*
Low (Commercial Viability)	**40 SOEs** [Consolidate & close down]	**3 SOEs** [Bulog, PLN, Taspen]
High (Commercial Viability)	**67 SOEs** [Consolidate & pursue non-state ownership]	**4 SOEs** [Jasa Tirta I & II, Pertamina, Inalum]

PLN = Perusahaan Listrik Negara, SOE = state-owned enterprise.

Note: The number of SOE reflects the 2019 total. Chapter XIV (Article 33, para. 2) of the 1945 Constitution states, "Sectors of production which are important for the country and affect the life of the people shall be controlled by the state." While this can be interpreted in various ways, it would seem to compel government or government-controlled entities to provide basic infrastructure services (and indeed a significant portion of overall infrastructure and infrastructure investment relates to SOEs). The Constitution also states in Article 33, para. 3, "The land, the waters and the natural resources within shall be under the powers of the State and shall be used to the greatest benefit of the people." This article has been used in general to justify state ownership of natural resource companies.

* In this figure, "unavoidable" SOEs are those operating in sectors where the state may be obliged by the constitution to provide services. Classification as "unavoidable" does not imply an endorsement of the need for SOEs in a given sector. The classification of "unavoidable" SOEs here largely follows that of Khatri and Ikhsan (2020), with differences due to the government's ongoing SOE consolidation process.

Source: Asian Development Bank (ADB) calculations using data from the Ministry of State-Owned Enterprises and Y. Khatri and M. Ikhsan. 2020. Enhancing the Development Contribution of Indonesia's State-Owned Enterprises. In E. Ginting and K. Naqvi, eds. *Reforms, Opportunities, and Challenges for State-Owned Enterprises*. Manila: ADB.

62.   **Identified Constraint II: Several viable and valuable state-owned enterprises should face more market incentives.** Several international frameworks emphasize the need for a clear rationale for state ownership, including those from the IMF, OECD, and the World Bank, as reviewed in Box 8. In line with the analysis presented in an ADB report drawing on the IMF framework (footnote 37), Figure 12 adds a consideration of SOEs that may be "unavoidable" to the commercial viability analysis presented in para. 29.[85] Only seven SOEs (Perum Bulog, PLN, Perum Jasa Tirta I and II, Pertamina, and PT Taspen) could be deemed "unavoidable" from the perspective of the obligations placed on the state on public service delivery by Indonesia's Constitution (further discussion is in Annex 3). As such, many SOEs in Indonesia may not possess a clear rationale for full state ownership, as assessed from a perspective guided by international best practices. Figure 12 offers a logical framework to assess SOEs as both commercial and development entities, while further and regular analysis are encouraged to inform policies given ongoing consolidation efforts.

---

[85]   "Unavoidable" SOEs is defined as those SOEs for which state ownership maybe justified under the Constitution of the Republic of Indonesia. Y. Khatri and M. Ikhsan. 2020. Enhancing the Development Contribution of Indonesia's State-Owned Enterprises. In E. Ginting and K. Naqvi, eds. *Reforms, Opportunities, and Challenges for State-Owned Enterprises*. Manila: ADB.

Box 8: International Perspectives on State-Owned Enterprises' Reform

Organisation for Economic Co-operation and Development Guidelines on Corporate Governance of State-Owned Enterprises. The 2015 edition of the Organisation for Economic Co-operation and Development's (OECD) state-owned enterprise (SOE) corporate governance guidelines, part of an influential series of recommendations first published in 2005, was developed with input from several developing countries (including Indonesia). The guidelines are recommendations to governments to ensure that SOEs "operate efficiently, transparently, and in an accountable manner."[a] A departure from the prior edition of the guidelines is an enumeration of potential rationales for state ownership, an acknowledgement that many developing state governments participate in the corporate sector through SOEs to support developmental goals. The guidelines recommend

(i)   exercising state ownership in the interest of the public, if state ownership is necessary;

(ii)   ensuring transparent and accountable governance of SOEs;

(iii)   establishing a level playing field between SOEs and private firms;

(iv)   ensuring that nongovernment shareholders of publicly listed SOEs receive equitable treatment and have equal access to corporate information;

(v)   providing clarity regarding expectations for responsible business conduct by SOEs and respecting shareholders' rights;

(vi)   setting high standards of transparency and disclosure for SOEs; and

(vii)   allowing boards of SOEs the necessary authority, competencies, and objectivity to carry out their functions and ensuring they are held accountable for their actions.

Organisation for Economic Co-operation and Development Guidelines on Anti-Corruption and Integrity in SOEs. Building on its main SOE guidelines, the OECD has also prepared several additional guidelines that provide recommendations on specific issues related to SOE governance. One such guideline document focuses on anti-corruption and integrity in SOEs, setting out recommendations for the state, for the exercise of state ownership, and for SOEs (aligning well with the three pillars used to frame the recommendations of this report), as well as for overall accountability.[b] These recommendations provide a useful lens for assessing governance risk in SOEs, and powerfully emphasize the need for the state to establish and support high standards of conduct and integrity while empowering independent, autonomous SOE boards.

(i)   Integrity of the state
    a.   Apply high standards of conduct to the state.
    b.   Establish ownership arrangements that are conducive to integrity.

(ii)   Exercise of state ownership for integrity
    a.   Ensure clarity in the legal and regulatory framework and in the state's expectations for anti-corruption and integrity.
    b.   Act as an active and informed owner with regard to anti-corruption and integrity in SOEs.

(iii)   Promotion of integrity and prevention at the enterprise level
    a.   Encourage integrated risk management systems in SOEs.
    b.   Promote internal controls, ethics, and compliance measures in SOEs.
    c.   Safeguard the autonomy of SOEs' decision-making bodies.

(iv)   Accountability of SOEs and of the state
    a.   Establish accountability and review mechanisms for SOEs.
    b.   Take action and respect due process for investigations and prosecutions.
    c.   Invite the inputs of civil society, the public and media, and the business community.

World Bank SOE Toolkit for the Corporate Governance of SOEs. Other organizations have also prepared guidelines for SOE governance and management. The World Bank's toolkit for the corporate governance of SOEs sets out seven chapters, several of which are closely related to those of the OECD guidelines.[c] The aim of corporate governance reforms should be to enhance the competitiveness of SOEs, provide critical goods, protect investments,

continued on next page

Box 8 *continued*

deliver services at a lower price, reduce the costs and risks of state ownership, and improve transparency and accountability. To achieve these goals, the World Bank recommends:

(i)   establishing a sound legal and regulatory framework for corporate governance;
(ii)   creating proper ownership arrangements for effective state oversight and enhanced accountability;
(iii)   developing a sound performance monitoring system;
(iv)   promoting financial and fiscal discipline;
(v)   professionalizing SOE boards;
(vi)   enhancing transparency and disclosure; and
(vii)   protecting shareholder rights in mixed-ownership companies.

International Monetary Fund State-Owned Enterprise framework. The International Monetary Fund's (IMF) fiscal policy note on financial oversight of SOEs complements the World Bank and OECD recommendations, arguing for clearly defined legal frameworks, transparency on government goals and SOE performance, and the need for capacity within the system of SOE oversight so that the institutions charged with overseeing SOEs have the high degree of competency needed to fulfil their role.[d] The IMF sets out a framework for identifying SOEs that struggle financially and/or lack a clear rationale for public ownership as key targets of reform, either for divestment, restructuring and repurposing, or consolidation based on the SOE's social and economic value. This classification aims to clarify when policy goals that are presently targeted through SOEs may be best achieved through other means. An analysis using this framework was adopted in the 2020 Asian Development Bank (ADB) report on SOEs in Indonesia, which highlights the large number of SOEs that lack a clear rationale for state ownership and struggle financially (this analysis is revisited later in this diagnostic in Figure 12).[e]

[a] OECD. 2015. *OECD Guidelines on Corporate Governance of State-Owned Enterprises*. Paris.
[b] OECD. 2019. *Guidelines on Anti-Corruption and Integrity in SOEs*. Paris.
[c] World Bank. 2014. *Corporate Governance of State-Owned Enterprises: A Toolkit*. Washington, DC.
[d] IMF. 2016. *Fiscal Policy: How to Improve the Financial Oversight of Public Corporations*. Washington, DC. November.
[e] E. Ginting and K. Naqvi, eds. *Reforms, Opportunities, and Challenges for State-Owned Enterprises*. Manila: ADB.
Source: Asian Development Bank.

63.   **Proposed Reform II: Encourage at least partial non-state ownership of commercially viable state-owned enterprises through initial public offerings or sales.** Once firms are consolidated, restructured, and made commercially viable, those SOEs that can have an IPO should be listed on the stock exchange (Figure 12) (footnote 12). Furthermore, efforts should be made to increase their exposure to market incentives to ensure that they are viable commercial entities with minimal state intervention in their operations, short of full divestment and privatization in cases where political economic constraints are binding. The experience of SOE privatization in Indonesia has highlighted the greater public acceptance of IPOs or rights issues in the capital market, as opposed to strategic sales.[86] Publicly listed SOEs face greater market incentives to perform, must abide by heightened transparency and auditing standards, and the minority investors in SOEs often push for the adoption of best practices in a number of areas such as gender representation and a greater focus on climate issues. As emphasized by stakeholders interviewed for this study, the risk of outside shareholders selling and pushing down company value also provides leverage for SOEs to better negotiate PSO requirements to ensure

[86] T. Praseniantono. 2004. Political Economy of Privatisation of State-Owned Enterprises in Indonesia. In M. C. Basri and P. v. d. Eng, eds. *Business in Indonesia: New Challenges, Old Problems*. ISEAS-Yusof Ishak Institute. Singapore.

that PSO compensation structures are appropriate. This study's analysis of public listing of SOEs highlights a correlation between listing and increased performance several years post-listing (para. 31). Encouraging at least partial nonstate ownership should be an initial priority of SOEs' reform.

64.   **Identified Constraint III: State-owned enterprises have limited autonomy and incentives for management to improve long-term performance.** SOEs must request approval from the MSOE for a variety of actions, and have limited scope to develop and execute business plans. SOE boards of directors, chief executive officers, and other members of top leadership are frequently reshuffled. Several stakeholders with experience in private firms have indicated that the rate of change of SOE leadership far exceeds that in the private sector (para. 33). This discourages managers from investing in improving SOE performance, and contributes to short-term planning within SOEs. SOE business plans are developed with guidance from the MSOE, but frequent changes in SOE leadership leading to changes in SOE strategic plans make it difficult to fulfill long-term plans. Leadership has often not been selected meritocratically, contributing to suboptimal performance even in companies with otherwise strong assets. Management has also historically not been representative of the population, with women accounting for just 1 in 10 board members (para. 41).

65.   **Proposed Reform III: Improve the quality of State-Owned Enterprises leadership and give State-Owned Enterprises boards more independence while increasing accountability for State-Owned Enterprises performance.** Those SOEs that are commercially viable should be allowed greater autonomy, in line with best practices for SOE governance. Increasing the professionalism and accountability of SOE boards to ensure that board members are qualified for their roles and have sufficient experience can enable SOEs to function more independently while allowing the MSOE to focus on its oversight role.[87] The MSOE must continue to play a role by setting governance policies and ensuring transparency, good governance, and selecting appropriate boards to oversee SOE operations (footnote 77). SOEs should have more ability to pursue investment opportunities, set long-term plans, and operate with autonomy to pursue objectives agreed with the MSOE, rather than be subject to micromanagement. SOEs should have more ability to hire, retain, and develop talent (including through support for executive education programs) in line with private sector practices, to enable SOEs to compete commercially with private firms. Increasing accountability, board stability, and board quality can enable SOEs to make better long-term plans, help enhance SOE performance, and improve MSOE oversight.

---

[87]   World Bank. 2006. *Held by the Visible Hand: The Challenge of SOE Corporate Governance for Emerging Markets.* Washington, DC.

VI. Conclusion

66.   SOEs' reform was a pressing concern for Indonesia prior to the COVID-19 pandemic, and the critical need to ensure a rapid economic recovery only increases the importance of tackling the persistent problems surrounding Indonesia's SOEs. SOEs were able to play a key role in the government's policy response. However, overstretched finances and the added strain of the pandemic present serious risks. Improving SOE governance by strengthening and refocusing the MSOE, minimizing the negative impacts of PSOs on SOEs by refining the relationship between SOEs and the government, and enabling SOEs with increased autonomy while pursuing partial privatization of viable firms and closures of unviable firms can enable SOEs to better deliver on their social mission and help support Indonesia's recovery.

67.   Enhancing the capacity of the MSOE while increasing its focus on establishing good governance practices is a necessary step in ensuring that SOEs perform well and mitigating several of the risks surrounding state ownership. Ensuring full implementation of the spirit of the SOE Law, by applying the high governance standards prescribed within it to the full SOE ecosystem, can help align Indonesia's SOE governance with best practices and address corruption and mismanagement concerns. Better cost assessment of PSOs, adopting subsidy structures that encourage more competition such as consumer subsidies, and ensuring that many current PSOs in infrastructure are compensated through viability gap funding rather than through equity injections can minimize the stresses of PSOs on SOEs, increase macroeconomic dynamism by reducing the distortions created by SOEs, and improve the delivery of public goods. For unviable SOEs that lack a clear rationale for state ownership, the MSOE should support closure and divestment. Other SOEs that are commercially viable and possess a rationale for state ownership should be exposed to at least partial nonstate ownership to increase their exposure to market incentives. The autonomy and independence of SOE boards should be respected by the MSOE, in line with the requirements of the SOE Law.

68.   Improving SOE performance and encouraging partial non-state ownership of SOEs can help increase the government's fiscal space to better address the requirements of the COVID-19 pandemic response as well as future needs. Initial public offerings or other public offerings for SOEs can provide the government with critical budgetary resources in the short term, while also helping support improved performance in the long term. Improved performance can in turn ensure increased tax payments, lower subsidies, and fewer equity injections to SOEs, reducing the costs of state ownership while increasing the contribution of SOEs to the state budget. Beyond pandemic recovery, these steps can help improve the sustainability of Indonesia's development. The growing debt of SOEs, signs of declining SOE performance, and increasing implicit subsidies going to SOEs all pose potential risks for Indonesia going forward. Mitigating these risks by addressing several of the constraints facing SOEs will have many benefits for Indonesia's economic dynamism.

Appendix 1
Line Ministries Impacting Sector State-Owned Enterprise Clusters

Table A1 shows a breakdown of the line and sector ministries with regulatory and other impacts on state-owned enterprises (SOEs) by each sector. The sector clusters here are based on the current Ministry of State-Owned Enterprises (MSOE) organization. All sector clusters are impacted by the MSOE (as oversight body) and the Ministry of Finance (MoF) as the ultimate owner of state assets and recipient of dividends.

Table A1: Line Ministries Impacting Sector State-Owned Enterprise Clusters

SECTOR CLUSTER	LINE AND SECTOR MINISTRIES
Energy, oil, and gas	Ministry of Energy and Mineral Resources
	Ministry of Industry
	Oil and Gas Regulatory Agency
Minerals and coal	Ministry of Energy and Mineral Resources
	Coordinating Ministry for Economic Affairs
	Coordinating Ministry for Maritime and Investment Affairs
Fertilizer and food	Ministry of Agriculture
	Ministry of Environment and Forestry
	Ministry of Industry
	Ministry of Maritime Affairs and Fisheries
	Ministry of Public Works and Public Housing
	Ministry of Trade
	Ministry of Transportation
	Coordinating Ministry for Economic Affairs
	Coordinating Ministry for Maritime and Investment Affairs
	Ministry of Cooperatives and Small and Medium Enterprises
	National Research and Innovation Agency
Plantations and forestry	Ministry of Agriculture
	Ministry of Environment and Forestry
	Ministry of Trade
	Ministry of Industry

continued on next page

Table A1 *continued*

SECTOR CLUSTER	LINE AND SECTOR MINISTRIES
Manufacturing (including defense)	Ministry of Defense
	Ministry of Industry
	Ministry of Trade
	Defense Industry Policy Committee
Health	Ministry of Health
Finance	Ministry of Cooperatives and Small and Medium Enterprises
	Coordinating Ministry for Economic Affairs
	Bank Indonesia
	Indonesia Deposit Insurance Corporation
	Financial Services Authority
	National Committee for Sharia Economics and Finance
Logistics	Ministry of Transportation
	Coordinating Ministry for Maritime and Investment Affairs
Infrastructure	Ministry of Energy and Mineral Resources
	Ministry of Public Works and Public Housing
	Ministry of Transportation
	Coordinating Ministry for Economic Affairs
	Coordinating Ministry for Maritime and Investment Affairs
Tourism and support	Ministry of Tourism and Creative Economy
	Ministry of Transportation
	Coordinating Ministry for Maritime and Investment Affairs
Insurance and pensions	Ministry of Defense
	Ministry of Transportation
	Coordinating Ministry for Economic Affairs
	Financial Services Authority
Telecommunications and media	Ministry of Communication and Information Technology
	Ministry of Education and Culture
	Ministry of Industry Indonesia
	Ministry of Law and Human Rights
	Ministry of Public Works and Public Housing
	Ministry of Tourism and Creative Economy
	Ministry of Transportation

Source: Government of Indonesia, Ministry of State-Owned Enterprises.

Appendix 2
State-Owned Enterprise Privatizations and Sales

Table A2 provides a listing of SOE privatizations in Indonesia since 1990. Sales carried out by the Indonesia Bank Restructuring Agency following the Asian financial crisis are excluded.

Table A2: State-Owned Enterprise Privatizations and Sales

Year	SOE	% Sold	Method	% Government, post
1991	Pt Semen Gresik[a]	35.00	IPO	65.00
1994	PT Indosat Tbk	35.00	IPO	65.00
1995	PT Tambang Timah Tbk	35.00	IPO	65.00
1995	PT Telkom Tbk	23.00	IPO	80.00
1996	PT BNI Tbk	25.00	IPO	75.00
1997	PT Aneka Tambang Tbk	35.00	IPO	65.00
1998	PT Semen Gresik[a]	14.00	Strategic sale	51.00
1999	PT Telkom Tbk	9.62	Placement	66.19
2001	PT Kimia Farma Tbk	9.20	IPO	90.80
2001	PT Indofarma Tbk	19.80	IPO	80.20
2001	PT Socfindo	30.00	Strategic sale	10.00
2001	PT Telkom Tbk	11.90	Placement	54.29
2002	PT Indosat Tbk	8.06	Placement	59.94
2002	PT Indosat Tbk	41.94	Strategic sale	14.39
2002	PT Telkom Tbk	3.10	Placement	51.19
2002	PT Tambang Batubara Bukit Asam Tbk	16.26	IPO	84.00
2002	PT WNI	41.99	Strategic sale	0
2003	PT Bank Mandiri Tbk	20.00	IPO	80.00
2003	PT Indocement TP Tbk	16.67	Strategic sale	0
2003	PT BRI Tbk	45.00	IPO	57.57
2003	PT PGN Tbk	39.00	IPO	60.03
2004	PT Pembangunan Perumahan Tbk	49.00	E/M buyout	51.00
2004	PT Adhi Karya Tbk	49.00	E/M buyout and IPO	51.00
2004	PT Bank Mandiri Tbk	10.00	Placement	69.96
2004	PT Tambang Batubara Bukit Asam Tbk	12.50	Sec. public offering	65.02
2006	PT PGN Tbk	5.31	Placement	55.33

continued on next page

Table A2 *continued*

Year	SOE	% Sold	Method	% Government, post
2007	PT BNI Tbk	26.30	Sec. public offering	76.36
2007	PT Jasa Marga Tbk	30.00	IPO	70.00
2007	PT Wijaya Karya Tbk	31.70	IPO	68.30
2009	PT BTN Tbk	27.08	IPO	72.92
2010	PT Pembangunan Perumahan Tbk	21.46	IPO	51.00
2010	PT Krakatau Steel Tbk	20.00	IPO	80.00
2010	PT BNI Tbk	21.20	Divestment/right issue	60.00
2010	PT Kertas Blabak	0.84	Strategic sale	0
2010	PT Intirub	9.99	Strategic sale	0
2011	PT Garuda Indonesia Tbk	26.67	IPO	69.14
2011	PT Bank Mandiri Tbk	10.12	Right issue	60.00
2011	PT Kertas Basuki Rachmat	0.38	Strategic sale	0
2011	PT Atmindo	36.65	Strategic sale	0
2011	PT Jakarta Int. Hotel Dev. Tbk	1.33	Drip Sale	0
2012	PT Waskita Karya (Persero) Tbk	32.00	IPO	68.00

E/M buyout = employee/management buyout, IPO = initial public offering, SOE = state-owned enterprise.

[a] Now PT Semen Indonesia (Persero) Tbk

Note: Privatizations under Indonesia Bank Restructuring Agency are not included.

Source: Government of Indonesia, Ministry of State-Owned Enterprises.

Appendix 3
Data Annex

A. State-Owned Enterprise Return on Equity and Implicit Subsidies

Using data from Damodaran Online, a comparison of state-owned enterprise (SOE) return on equity (ROE) and emerging market average ROE was constructed.[1] Each of the 114 SOEs in 2019 was assigned to one of the industries in the Damodaran data and an average ROE for Indonesian SOEs in each sector over the period 2015 to 2019 was calculated. This was then compared against an average ROE for emerging markets over this period. The study concentrated on 2015 onward due to large revaluations in SOE assets that occurred in 2014.

The method for calculating implicit subsidies builds on earlier work that compared SOEs against a single benchmark ROE to calculate an implicit subsidy.[2] Rather than use one flat benchmark rate for the comparison ROE for all sectors, the study built on the emerging market average ROEs by sector and by year as reported in the Damodaran database. As ROE varies substantially by sector and over time, this allowed a more accurate computation of estimates of implicit subsidies.

$$ImplicitSubsidy_{ij} = Profit_{ij} - \left[Equity_{ij} * SectorROE_j \right]$$

The implicit subsidy for SOE (i) in year (j) is given by the profits of SOE (i) in year (j) minus SOE (i) equity in year (j) times the average emerging market SOE for the sector of SOE (i) in year (j). This revised estimate incorporates differences in performance across sectors and over time.

B. Viability of State-Owned Enterprises

The assessment of viability is adapted from an Asian Development Bank (ADB) report on Indonesian SOEs.[3] "Viability" is defined as (i) achieving an ROE of one-half of the emerging market average ROE for its sector in at least 3 of 5 years from 2015–2019, using emerging market average ROE by sector and year as reported in the Damodaran database, and (ii) achieving a positive return of asset (ROA) over the 5-year period from 2015 to 2019. ROE was winsorized at ±25%. Years when SOEs reported negative equity were excluded from the calculation.

[1] Damodaran Online. Data: Current and Data: Archives (accessed January 2021).
[2] AIPEG. Implicit Subsidies to Indonesia's SOEs are creating significant risks to Indonesia's economy. Unpublished; E. Ginting and K. Naqvi, eds. 2020. *Reforms, Opportunities, and Challenges for State-Owned Enterprises*. Manila: ADB.
[3] Y. Khatri and M. Ikhsan. 2020. Enhancing the Development Contribution of Indonesia's State-Owned Enterprises. In E. Ginting and K. Naqvi, eds. *Reforms, Opportunities, and Challenges for State-Owned Enterprises*. Manila: ADB.

Likewise, "unavoidable" SOEs is also defined based on the study by Ikhsan and Khatri (Footnote 3). "Unavoidable" SOEs are those where state ownership may be justified under the Constitution of the Republic of Indonesia. The report states that Chapter XIV (Article 33, para. 2) of the 1945 Constitution states, "Sectors of production which are important for the country and affect the life of the people shall be controlled by the state." While this can be interpreted in various ways, it would seem to compel government or government-controlled entities to provide basic infrastructure services (and indeed a significant portion of overall infrastructure and infrastructure investment relates to SOEs). The Constitution also states in Article 33, para. 3, "The land, the waters and the natural resources within shall be under the powers of the State and shall be used to the greatest benefit of the people." This article has been used in general to justify state ownership of natural resource companies. The difference in the number of SOEs between this diagnostic and ADB 2020 is due to the recent consolidations of SOEs.

C. Performance and Public Listing Analysis

Data overview. The MSOE generously allowed access to its records on SOE performance during 2000–2019. Data shared with the study includes a range of key financial indicators for the whole period including SOE assets, liabilities, equity, net profit, as well as a broader set of indicators such as dividends and taxes paid to the government, input costs, capital spending, and cash flow over the 2010–2019 period. Where possible, these data have been cross-checked with data collected from the Orbis database of Bureau Van Dijk.[4] With these data, we are able to complete novel analyses of the impact of reform on SOE performance, as well as of the potential impacts of future reform on government finances.

ROA is calculated simply as the net profit of the SOE over its assets. ROE requires adjustments for instances where firm equity is low or negative, which can lead to inflated ROE numbers or (when profits and equity are both negative) misleading figures. To address these concerns, SOEs from the sample when they report negative equity or an equity-assets ratio of less than 0.05 were excluded. ROE was winsorized at 25% and –25% for the remaining SOEs.

Regression Framework. The following equation was used to investigate the impact of traded shares on SOE performance:

$$ROA_{ij} = \beta_0 + ShareTraded_{ij-5} + \beta_2 Assets_{ij} + \delta_1 YearFE_j + \delta_2 FixedEffects_i + \in$$

In equation 1, ROA_ij represents the ROA of each SOE (i) in each year (j), $ShareTraded\_ij-5$ represents the share of each SOE's shares that are publicly traded (lagged 5 years), and $Assets\_ij$ represents the log of SOE's assets measured as a share of GDP (alternative methods of controlling for assets return similar results). The prior percent of shares traded, $ShareTraded\_ij-5$ (5 years prior) was used, as it may take time for additional publicly traded shares to impact SOE performance. This also mitigates (but does not eliminate) concerns that the opposite relationship (that better performance leads to more listed shares) could be driving the results, by looking at the link between firm performance and traded shares in a prior period. In some specifications the sample was restricted to only those firms that have undergone an initial public offering (IPO) or change in shareholding over the period, including firm-level fixed effects, with standard errors clustered at the firm level (to use firm-level fixed effects, firm-level variation in the percentage of publicly traded shares was required).

4   Bureau Van Dijk. 2021. Orbis Database. Brussels (accessed January 2021).

This framework was then modified to allow the impact of publicly traded shares to vary depending on the size of SOE by adding an interaction term between SOE assets and the percentage of SOE shares which are publicly traded. Several stakeholders expressed a sense that IPOs were more impactful for large SOEs, as they were more attractive for the market. This specification is reflected in equation 2, where DDD represents the interaction term:

$$ROA_{ij} = \beta_o + \beta_1 ShareTraded_{ij-5} + \beta_2 Assets_{ij} + \beta_3 ShareTraded_{ij-5} XAssets_{ij}$$
$$\delta_1 YearFE_j + \delta_2 FixedEffects_i + \in$$

Analysis framework. The study began by analyzing the impact of IPOs and non-government shareholding on SOE performance. This analysis focused on the 50 largest SOEs in 2019, which accounted for more than 98% of SOE assets in that year, using data from 2000 to 2019. The study focused on this subset of SOEs to exclude smaller SOEs, many of which are in restructuring, are nonperforming, or are economically insignificant. Focusing on a consistent set of SOEs over this time period also allows for more precise analysis of the role of privatization, as many of these SOEs had an IPO over this period and data for this set of SOEs for an average of 17.1 years for each SOE over this 20-year period (for ROA) were available.

Robustness checks. Table A3.1 below relaxes the sample selection used for the table presented in the main text. All SOEs for which we have data are included in the columns without firm fixed effects, and with firm fixed effects the sample includes all SOEs with at least some publicly traded shares over the period. The results are largely the same, with similar magnitudes, with the exception of column 3. In column 3, traded shares are associated with declining ROA for larger SOEs. We do not feel that this difference between the specifications should be given too much weight, as the specification in column 3 is not as representative of the impact of SOE privatization as those in columns including firm effects.

Table A3.1: Full Sample, State-Owned Enterprise Privatization and Performance

	ROA				ROE			
	(1)	(2)	(3)	(4)	(5)	(6)	(7)	(8)
% Traded (prior)	0.140***	0.0571	-0.103	0.230**	0.116***	0.0456	0.251***	0.202**
	(0.0248)	(0.0387)	(0.0746)	(0.0814)	(0.0170)	(0.0492)	(0.0512)	(0.0872)
Ln(Assets, % GDP)	0.00377**	0.00734	0.00469***	0.00684	0.00679***	-0.00715	0.00619***	-0.00808
	(0.00165)	(0.00875)	(0.00171)	(0.00764)	(0.00144)	(0.0103)	(0.00154)	(0.00965)
% Traded (prior) X			-0.0433***	0.0318**			0.0240***	0.0286**
Ln(Assets, % GDP)			(0.0144)	(0.0122)			(0.00856)	(0.0133)
Year FE	Yes	Yes	Yes	Yes	Yes	Yes	Yes	Yes
Firm FE		Yes		Yes		Yes		Yes
Std. Error Cluster		Yes (firm)		Yes (firm)		Yes (firm)		Yes (firm)
Adj. R2	0.014	0.569	0.016	0.574	0.059	0.566	0.059	0.569
N	2434	370	2434	370	2084	359	2084	359

Notes.

1. Standard errors in parentheses, * p<0.10, ** p<0.05, *** p<0.01.

2. In Columns 2, 4, 6, and 8 standard errors are clustered by firm and the sample includes only firms with nongovernment shareholding from 2000–2019.

GDP = gross domestic product, ROA = return on asset, ROE = return on equity, SOE = state-owned enterprise.

Source: Asian Development Bank calculations using Ministry of State-Owned Enterprises data.

continued on next page

We can adjust the framework to include sector fixed effects rather than firm fixed effects.[5] To ensure variation within a sector in the traded share of firms, the sample was limited to only SOEs operating in sectors with some traded shares. The results of this regression are shown in Table A3.2. None of the specifications return a statistically significant result, and results are also not significant when the sample is restricted to the top 50 largest SOEs.

Table A3.2: Full Sample, Sector Fixed Effects, State-Owned Enterprise Privatization and Performance

	ROA		ROE	
	(1)	(2)	(3)	(4)
% Traded (prior)	0.0531	0.0978	0.0440	0.369
	(0.0788)	(0.236)	(0.0748)	(0.261)
Ln(Assets, % GDP)	0.00356	0.00323	0.00788	0.00494
	(0.0111)	(0.0112)	(0.0108)	(0.0116)
% Traded (prior) X		0.00829		0.0597
Ln(Assets, % GDP)		(0.0337)		(0.0365)
Year FE	Yes	Yes	Yes	Yes
Sector FE	Yes	Yes	Yes	Yes
Std. Error Cluster	Yes (Sector)	Yes (Sector)	Yes (Sector)	Yes (Sector)
Adj. R2	0.039	0.038	0.153	0.165
N	817	817	765	765

Notes.

1. Standard errors in parentheses, * p<0.10, ** p<0.05, *** p<0.01.

2. All errors are clustered by sector and the sample includes only firms in sectors with at least one firm with nongovernment shareholding from 2000–2019.

GDP = gross domestic product, ROA = return on asset, ROE = return on equity, SOE = state-owned enterprise.

Source: Asian Development Bank calculations using Ministry of State-Owned Enterprises data.

Despite these null results and minor differences with the main regression presented in the paper, the preferred results using firm fixed effects are robust. The study observed a positive result in columns 4 and 8 of Tables A3.1 and A3.2, indicative of a robust correlation between increased privatization and better firm performance.

D. Performance in Manufacturing, using IBS Data

Data. As noted in para. 29, SOE manufacturing firms often perform poorly. Many of the 34 SOEs under the management of the two state companies tasked with restructuring and strengthening struggling SOEs are manufacturing firms.[6] Struggles within this sector can be confirmed using data from the *Survei Industri Besar dan Sedang* (Large and Medium-Scale Manufacturing Survey, or IBS survey), which captures all manufacturing firms (including SOE subsidiaries) with more than 20 employees on an annual basis. The study used data from these surveys from 2000–2015, and restricted the sample to central government SOEs (excluding local government

---

[5]   These include the 12 current sectors defined by the Ministry of State-Owned Enterprises, while categorizing SOEs being restructured or otherwise under the management of the state asset-management companies (Danareksa and . Perusahaan Pengelola Aset [PPA]) as a "13th" sector (when interviewed, ministry officials adopted this characterization of SOEs under management as a separate sector). The sectors are: (i) insurance and pensions, (ii) energy, (iii) infrastructure, (iv) financial services, (v) health, (vi) logistics, (vii) manufacturing, (viii) minerals and coal, (ix) food and fertilizer, (x) tourism, (xi) agriculture and forestry, (xii) telecommunications and media, and (xiii) miscellaneous under Danareksa/PPA management.

[6]   E. Ginting and K. Naqvi, eds. 2020. *Reforms, Opportunities, and Challenges for State-Owned Enterprises.* Manila: ADB.

SOEs, which are not the subject of this paper) and privately owned firms (including international ownership). This data is often, but not always, reported at the subsidiary level. Some of the largest SOEs in the IBS data include PT Krakatau Steel (a steel producer), PT Pupuk subsidiary Petrokimia Gresik (a fertilizer company), and PT Perkebunan subsidiary Pabrik Gula Cinta Manis (a sugar factory).

Productivity was measured as the ratio between a firm's inputs and its outputs. Similarly, productivity per worker was measured as the ratio between a firm's outputs and the number of employees of that firm. As some data in the IBS survey is misreported, missing or withheld, which can lead to unusually high or low measures of productivity, the productivity ratio is restricted to values within 2.0 and 0.5 (a firm reporting output valued at twice inputs or inputs valued at twice outputs).

Regression framework. The study used the following equation to investigate the impact of traded shares on SOE performance:

$$Productivity_{ij} = \beta_o + \beta_1 SOE_i + \delta_1 YearFE_j + \delta_2 FixedEffects_i + \in$$

Where $Productivity\_ij$ is either firm or worker productivity, SOE_i captures if firm i is an SOE, and fixed effects are included for the year and the product code of the firm. Product codes are based on the reported International Standard Industrial Classification (ISIC) codes of the firm matched over the two ISIC revisions reported (ISIC 3 prior to 2010, and ISIC 4 in 2010 and after).

Table A3.3:   Manufacturing State-Owned Enterprises and Private Firm Performance Comparison

	Log of Firm Productivity (output/input)	Log of Worker Productivity (output/worker)
	(1)	(2)
SOE (dummy var.)	-0.0141*	-0.468***
	(0.00771)	(0.129)
Ln(Output)	0.0147***	0.538***
	(0.00117)	(0.0343)
Year FE	Yes	Yes
ISIC Code FE	Yes	Yes
Std. Err. Clustering	Yes (ISIC Code)	Yes (ISIC Code)
N	308,357	308,357

Notes.
1. Standard errors in parentheses, * p<0.10, ** p<0.05, *** p<0.01.
2. Standard errors are clustered by ISIC code.
ISIC = International Standard Industrial Classification, SOE = state-owned enterprise, FE = Fixed Effect.
Source: Asian Development Bank calculations using data from Survei Industri Besar dan Sedang (IBS Survey).

Using data from these surveys from 2000–2015, a comparison of the performance of SOEs and private firms in terms of their firm productivity (efficiency in turning inputs into outputs) and their labor productivity (output per worker) finds that SOEs perform roughly 1.4% worse in terms of firm productivity and 46.8% worse in terms of labor productivity (0).

Figure A4: Ministry of State-Owned Enterprises Organizational Structure, 2019

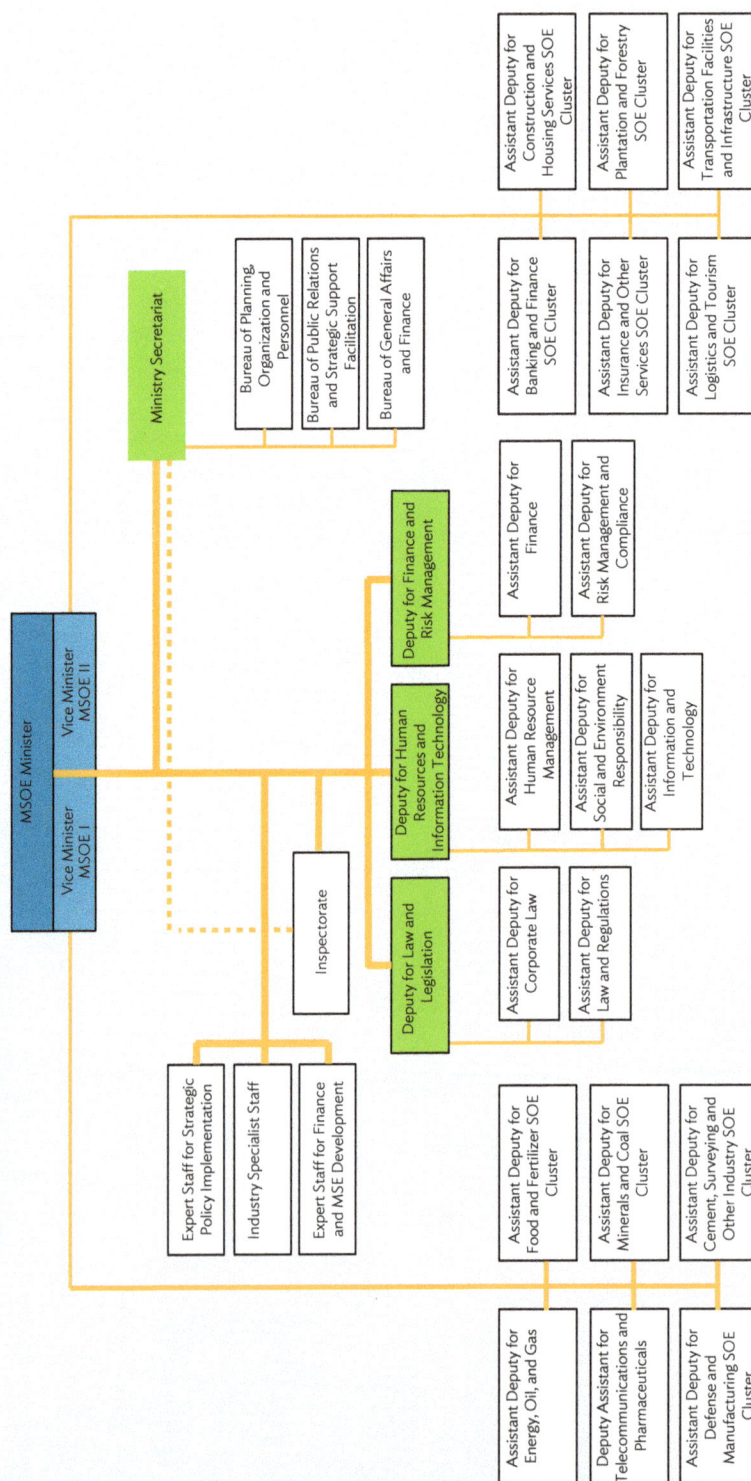

MSOE = Ministry of State-Owned Enterprises, SOE = state-owned enterprise.

Note: This structure has been in place since 2019.

Source: Government of Indonesia, Ministry of State-Owned Enterprises.

Appendix 5
Required Approvals

Table A5 outlines approvals required of a large, publicly listed state-owned enterprise (SOE). Requirements for all SOEs differ slightly, but the below is a representative example.

Table A5: Required Approvals for State-Owned Enterprises

Action	
Appointing and dismissing Board of Directors and Board of Commissioners	
Taking other actions that have not been stipulated in the Corporate Budget Plan	
Establishing organizational plan of the company	
Changing company logo	
Creating new positions and setting salaries	
Establishing foundations, organizations and/or associations, either directly or indirectly related to the company; imposing expenses that are fixed and routine for foundations, organizations and/or associations to the company, either directly or indirectly related to the company	
Action	**Threshold**
To release/transfer and/or pledge the assets of the company, except for inventory	> 50% Total assets
Cooperating with business entities or other parties, in the form of operational cooperation, business cooperation, licensing cooperation, build-operate-transfer, build-transfer-operate, build-operate-own, and other agreements that have the same nature	> 50% Total assets and length > 20
Making investments, releasing participation and changing the capital structure of other companies	> 5% Equity
Establishing a subsidiary and/or joint venture company	> 5% Equity
Carrying out a merger, consolidation, acquisition, separation, dissolution of subsidiaries and joint ventures, including equity participation in others through subsidiaries	> 5% Equity
Binding the company as guarantor	> 50% Equity
Receiving medium-/long-term loans and providing operational medium-/long-term loans	> 50% Equity
Providing short-/medium-/long-term non-operational nature, except loans to subsidiaries	> 50% Equity
Eliminating bad debt and inanimate inventory	> 50% Equity
Proposing company representatives to become candidates for members of the board of directors and board of commissioners in subsidiaries that make significant contributions to the company and/or have strategic value as determined by the board of commissioners	> 5% Consolidated total assets

Source: Government of Indonesia, Ministry of State-Owned Enterprises

Indonesia Compared against Organisation for Economic Co-operation and Development Guidelines for State-Owned Enterprise Governance

Table A6 highlights areas where Indonesia's state-owned enterprise (SOE) governance diverges from the guidelines of the Organisation for Economic Co-operation and Development on SOE corporate governance. Note that under each recommendation heading are areas where Indonesia's governance framework deviates from the recommendation (per the full text of the recommendations in the respective reports).

Table A6: Comparison of Indonesia State-Owned Enterprise Governance with the Organisation for Economic Co-operation and Development Guidelines

OECD
BETTER POLICIES FOR BETTER LIVES

Guidelines on Corporate Governance of SOEs

I. Rationales for state ownership
- Some SOEs lack a clear rationale for state ownership, should be candidates for divestment or closure

II. The state's role as an owner
- SOEs lack operational autonomy and board independence is not respected
- MSOE lacks capacity, competencies suited to its role
- SOE board and leadership selection should be more systematized

III. State-owned enterprises in the marketplace
- Public projects often not competitive, with SOEs often assigned projects
- PSO costs not accurately reported, fully funded, or paid on time

IV. Equitable treatment of shareholders and other investors
- Improved disclosure of PSOs, reflecting true cost, to nongovernment shareholders
- Ensuring minority shareholder representation on board where applicable

V. Stakeholder relations & responsible business
- SOE boards could improve standards, internal controls (corruption concerns)

VI. Disclosure & transparency
- Data should be standardized and collection improved (particularly for small SOEs)
- PSOs (and impact) should be accurately disclosed (reflecting full cost of PSO)

VII. Responsibilities of boards of SOEs
- More transparency needed in board nomination process, more professionalism
- Board should be responsible for planning, have more power and independence

MSOE = Ministry of State-Owned Enterprises, OECD = Organisation for Economic Co-operation and Development, PSO = public service obligation, SOE = state-owned enterprise.

Source: ADB, based on OECD. 2015. *OECD Guidelines on Corporate Governance of State-Owned Enterprises*. Paris.

References

Afifa, L. 2021. Minister Erick Thohir Aims to Boost Women's Leadership in SOEs. *Tempo*. 7 April. Jakarta.

Akhlas, A. W. 2020. SOEs to Receive Rp 40t Injection in 2021, Support Economic Recovery. *The Jakarta Post*. 9 November. Jakarta.

Asian Development Bank (ADB). 2008. *Completion Report: State-Owned Enterprise Governance and Privatization Program in Indonesia*. Manila.

ADB. 2015. *Fossil Fuels Subsidies in Indonesia: Trends, Impacts, Reforms*. Manila.

_____. 2018. *Strategy 2030: Achieving a Prosperous, Inclusive, Resilient, and Sustainable Asia and the Pacific*. Manila.

_____. 2018. *State-Owned Enterprise Engagement and Reform*. Manila.

_____. 2020. *Innovate Indonesia: Unlocking Growth through Technological Transformation*. Manila.

_____. 2020. *Country Partnership Strategy: Indonesia, 2020–2024—Emerging Stronger*. Inclusive and Sustainable Growth Assessment (accessible from the list of linked documents in Appendix 3). Manila

_____. 2020. *Country Partnership Strategy: Indonesia, 2020–2024—Emerging Stronger*. Manila.

_____. 2020. *Indonesia Energy Sector Assessment, Strategy, and Road Map—Update*. Manila.

_____. 2021. *Guidance Note on State-Owned Enterprise Reform in Sovereign Projects and Programs*. Manila.

Asian Development Bank Institute (ADBI). 2017. *Efficient Management of State-Owned Enterprises: Challenges and Opportunities*. Tokyo.

ADBI. 2020. *Enhancing the Transparency and Accountability of SOEs*. Tokyo.

Australia Indonesia Partnership for Economic Governance (AIPEG). Implicit Subsidies to Indonesia's SOEs are Creating Significant Risks to Indonesia's Economy. Unpublished.

AIPEG. The Fertilizer Sector and Subsidy Policy in Indonesia. Unpublished.

Bahfein, S. 2021. Adhi Karya Berambisi Rajai Sektor Konstruksi Kereta Api di Indonesia (Adhi Karya Aims to Dominate the Railway Construction Sector in Indonesia). *Kompas*. 1 May.

Bardan, A. B. 2021. Ada Yang Tidak Beres, Jokowi Minta Subsidi Pupuk Dievaluasi (Something's Not Right – Jokowi Asks for the Fertilizer Subsidy to be Evaluated). *Kontan*. 11 January. Jakarta.

Breue, L. E., J. Guajardo, and T. Kinda. 2018. *Realizing Indonesia's Economic Potential*. International Monetary Fund (IMF).

BUMN. 2020. Jakarta.

Cabrera, P., J. Oriol, and C. Moskovits. 2020. Valuation of Credit Guarantees to State-Owned Enterprises. Washington, DC.: Inter-American Development Bank.

Chang, H. J. 2007. State-Owned Enterprise Reform. National Development Strategies Policy Note. United Nations Department for Economic and Social Affairs.

Damodaran Online. Accessed January 2021.

Dorimulu, P. and M. F. Bona. 2021. Indonesia Administers Sinovac Vaccine Manufactured by Bio Farma. *Jakarta Globe*. 19 February.

Estrin, S. and A. Pelletier. 2018. Privatization in Developing Countries: What Are the Lessons of Recent Experience. *World Bank Research Observer*. 33 (1). pp. 65–102. February. Washington, DC.

Fitch Ratings. 2020. Compensation Delays to Pressurise PLN's Standalone Credit Profile. New York.

Ginting, E. 2003. The State Finance Law: Overlooked and Undervalued. *Bulletin of Indonesian Economic Studies*. 39 (3). pp. 353–357.

Ginting, E. and K. Naqvi, eds. 2020. *Reforms, Opportunities, and Challenges for State-Owned Enterprises*. Manila: ADB.

Government of Indonesia. KBUMN Annual Report 2015. Jakarta.

_____ 1945. Constitution. Jakarta.

_____ 2003. SOE Law (19/2003). Jakarta.

_____ 2003. State Finance Law (17/2003). Jakarta.

_____ 2004. Act of the Republic of Indonesia (1/2004) Concerning State Treasury. Jakarta.

_____ 2009. Law of the Republic of Indonesia Concerning Electricity (30/2009). Jakarta.

_____ 2019. National Medium-Term Development Plan 2020–2024. Jakarta.

_____ 2021. Keputusan Presiden (KEPPRES) 2/2021 (Amendment to Presidential Decree Number 47 of 2014 concerning the Public Company [Persero] Privatization Committee). Jakarta.

Government of Indonesia, Cabinet Secretariat. 2020. President Jokowi Pushes for Simplification of Bureaucracy. Jakarta.

Government of Indonesia, Cabinet Secretariat. 2020. 12 SOEs to Receive Stimulus as Part of Economic Recovery Programs. Jakarta.

Government of Indonesia, Ministry of Finance. 2020. BUMN Juga Masuk Program Pemulihan Ekonomi Nasional (SOEs Are Also a Part of the National Economic Recovery Program). Jakarta.

Government of Indonesia, Ministry of State-Owned Enterprises (MSOE). 2010. Master Plan Badan Usaha Milik Negara 2010–2014 (SOE Master Plan 2010–2014). Jakarta.

Government of Indonesia, MSOE. 2010. Roadmap BUMN 2015–2019. Jakarta.

_____ 2020. Profil Organisasi (Organization Profile). Jakarta.

Gumelar, G. 2020. Jiwasraya: Understanding Indonesia's Largest Financial Scandal. The Jakarta Post. 26 October.

Hanggi, H. 2020. Bio Farma to Receive Rp2 Trillion in State Capital Injections. Tempo. 6 November.

Hardiyan, Y. 2015. Telkom Bakal Gandeng Singtel Bentuk Usaha Patungan (Telkom to Cooperate with Singtel to Form a Joint Venture). Bisnis. 22 June.

Hill, H. 2000. Indonesia: The Strange and Sudden Death of a Tiger Economy. Oxford Development Studies. 28 (2). pp. 117–139.

Independent Evaluation Department. 2009. Validation Report: State-Owned Enterprise Governance and Privatization Program in Indonesia. Manila: ADB.

Indonesia Stock Exchange. 2004. Rule I-E Concerning the Obligation of Information Submission. Jakarta.

Indreswari, M. 2006. Corporate Governance of Indonesian State-Owned Enterprises. Thesis presented for the degree of Doctor Philosophy in Development Studies at Massey University, Palmerston North, New Zealand.

IMF. 1998. Indonesia Letter of Intent, 13 November. Jakarta.

_____ 2016. Fiscal Policy: How to Improve the Financial Oversight of Public Corporations. Washington, DC.

_____ 2019. Article IV Consultation 2019. Washington, DC.

Institute for Essential Services Reform. 2019. Indonesia's Coal Dynamics: Toward a Just Energy Transition. Jakarta.

The Jakarta Post. 2020. Ministry to Limit SOEs' Expert Staff Numbers, Salaries. 8 September.

_____ 2021. Indonesia Launches EV Battery Holding Company. 29 March.

Januarita, R. 2010. Equal Opportunities between SOEs and Private Companies. Bandung: Organisation for Economic Co-operation and Development (OECD).

Kim, K. 2018. Matchmaking: Establishment of State-Owned Holding Companies in Indonesia. *Journal of Asia & The Pacific Policy Studies*. 5 (2). pp. 313–330.

Kompas. 2021. Erick Thohir akan Lakukan Swastanisasi BUMN yang Pendapatannya di Bawah Rp 50 Miliar (Erick Thohir Will Privatize SOEs with Incomes Below Rp 50 Billion). 5 March.

MDI Ventures. About Us.

OECD. 2012. *Competitive Neutrality: Maintaining a Level Playing Field Between Public and Private Business*. Paris.

———. 2015. *Indonesia Policy Brief: Agriculture*. Paris.

———. 2015. *OECD Guidelines on Corporate Governance of State-Owned Enterprises*. Paris.

———. 2019. *Guidelines on Anti-Corruption and Integrity in State-Owned Enterprises*. Paris.

———. 2018. *Ownership and Governance of SOEs: A Compendium of National Practices*. Paris

———. 2021. OECD Economic Surveys: Indonesia. Paris.

———. 2020. *Transparency Frameworks for SOEs in Asia*. Paris.

Osorio, C. G. et al. 2011. Who is Benefiting from the Fertilizer Subsidies in Indonesia? *Policy Research Working Paper* 5758. Washington, DC.: World Bank.

Parama, M. and R. Rahman. 2020. House Approves Rp 8.5t in Convertible Bond for Ailing Garuda. *The Jakarta Post*. July 16.

Pertamina. MyPertamina.

PLN. 2020. *PLN Statistics 2019*. Jakarta.

Praseniantono, T. 2004. Political Economy of Privatisation of State-Owned Enterprises in Indonesia. In M. C. Basri and P. v. d. Eng, eds. *Business in Indonesia: New Challenges, Old Problems*. Singapore: ISISEAS-Yusof Ishak Institute.

Rahman, D. F. 2021. PLN Pledges Carbon Neutrality by 2050. *The Jakarta Post*. 8 May.

Rahman, R. 2020. Two Directors Lose Jobs over Investment Losses at State-Owned Asabri. *The Jakarta Post*. 30 January.

Rayess, M. E. et al. 2019. Indonesia's Public Wealth: A Balance Sheet Approach to Fiscal Policy Analysis. *IMF Working Paper*. No. 19/81. Washington, DC.

Richter, A. 2021. Plans on Merging State-Owned Geothermal Companies in Indonesia Back on the Table. *Think GeoEnergy*. 7 February.

Sari, S. A. and T. F. Tjoe. 2017. Board Remuneration and Good Corporate Governance in Indonesian State-owned Enterprises. *Global Business Review*. 18 (4). pp. 861–875.

Sato, Y. 2004. Bank Restructuring and Financial Institution Reform in Indonesia. *The Developing Economies*. 43 (1). pp. 91–120.

Shumkov, I. 2020. Masdar, PLN Unit Set Up JV to Tackle Floating Solar Development in Indonesia. *Renewables Now*. 17 December.

Simorangkir, E. 2017. Kembangkan Teknologi Konstruksi, Wika Belajar dari Jepan (Developing Construction Technology, Wika Learns from Japan). *DetikFinance*. 22 July.

Sjahrir. 1990. The Indonesian Economy Facing the 1990s. *Southeast Asian Affairs*. pp. 117–131.

Tani, S. 2021. Indonesian State Companies Set Up EV Battery Developer. *NikkeiAsia*. 27 March.

Tehusijarana, K. M. 2019. "The Main Thing is Not the Process But the Result": Jokowi's Full Inaugural Speech. *Jakarta Post*.

Temasek. Who We Are: About Us.

Tempo. 2012. Wika Gandeng Jepang Bangun MRT di Jakarta (Wika Collaborates with Japan to Build MRT in Jakarta). 10 May.

Wicaksono, A. 2008. Indonesian State-Owned Enterprises: The Challenge of Reform. *Southeast Asian Affairs*. pp. 146–167.

Worang, F. G. and D. A. Holloway. 2007. Corporate Governance in Indonesian State-Owned Enterprises. *Journal of Corporate Ownership & Control*. 4 (2). pp. 205–215.

World Bank. Infrastructure Sector Assessment. Unpublished.

———. 1995. Bureaucrats in Business Database. Washington, DC.

———. 2006. *Held by the Visible Hand: The Challenge of SOE Corporate Governance for Emerging Markets*. Washington, DC.

———. 2014. *Corporate Governance of State-Owned Enterprises: A Toolkit*. Washington, DC.

———. 2020. Indonesia Public Expenditure Review 2020: Spending for Better Results. Jakarta.

Yap, J., D. Tan, and L. Z. Yong. 2020. Corporate Governance In Indonesia – What You Need To Know About The Board Of Directors And Board Of Commissioners. *Mondaq*. 26 March.

www.ingramcontent.com/pod-product-compliance
Lightning Source LLC
Chambersburg PA
CBHW061221270326
41926CB00032B/4810